The Easy Yoke

Doug Webster

NAVPRESS
BRINGING TRUTH TO LIFE
NavPress Publishing Group
P.O. Box 35001, Colorado Springs, Colorado 80935

The Navigators is an international Christian organization. Jesus Christ gave His followers the Great Commission to go and make disciples (Matthew 28:19). The aim of The Navigators is to help fulfill that commission by multiplying laborers for Christ in every nation.

NavPress is the publishing ministry of The Navigators. NavPress publications are tools to help Christians grow. Although publications alone cannot make disciples or change lives, they can help believers learn biblical discipleship, and apply what they learn to their lives and ministries.

©1995 by Doug Webster

Library of Congress Catalog Card Number: 95-10095
ISBN 08910-99042

Some of the anecdotal illustrations in this book are true to life and are included with the permission of the persons involved. All other illustrations are composites of real situations, and any resemblance to people living or dead is coincidental.

Unless otherwise identified, all Scripture quotations in this publication are taken from the *HOLY BIBLE: NEW INTERNATIONAL VERSION®* (NIV®). Copyright © 1973, 1978, 1984 by International Bible Society. Used by permission of Zondervan Publishing House. All rights reserved. Another version used is *The Message: New Testament with Psalms and Proverbs* by Eugene H. Peterson, copyright © 1993, 1995, used by permission of NavPress Publishing Group.

Webster, Douglas D.
    The easy yoke / Doug Webster.
        p. cm.
    Includes bibliographical references.
    ISBN 0-89109-904-2
    1. Sermon on the mount—Criticism, interpretation, etc.
2. Christian life. I. Title.
BT380.2.W42 1995
241.5′3—dc20   95-10095
                                                        CIP

Printed in the United States of America

1 2 3 4 5 6 7 8 9 10/99 98 97 96 95

CONTENTS

To Daniel and Grace Lam,
who have given their all for the Kingdom

PREFACE

I wrote this book out of empathy for those who feel confused about what is expected of them as followers of Jesus. I also wrote it out of frustration with those who are taking advantage of sincere believers, by misrepresenting and distorting what is involved in living for Christ. In the effort to make Christianity more appealing and easier to accept, we often make it more difficult. People wonderfully saved by the grace of Christ are swept up into religious practices that rob them of the joy of following the Lord Jesus. Their identity and priorities are confused. Their understanding of the nature of righteousness is skewed, and their life-goals have more to do with personal ambition than a passion for Christ. My personal aim is to offer a clear picture of authentic, Jesus-style spirituality.

Many believers are tired of predictable formulas for spiritual success that are no match for the harsh realities of living for Christ in today's culture. They are ready for a fresh hearing of God's Word on what it means to follow Jesus. When years of religion and church attendance don't add up to deeper dependence on God, ethical maturity, and authentic spirituality, it is time for us to reexamine Jesus' expectations. In the Sermon on the Mount, Jesus invites us to move beyond tradition-bound religion and the shallow answers that don't work. He calls us to consider the cost of nondiscipleship.

Jesus' challenge, "Take up your cross daily and follow me," does not seem to fit His invitation, "Take my yoke upon you . . . for my yoke is easy and my burden is light." Yet the cost of discipleship and the easy yoke go together perfectly. This book takes a close look at the Sermon on the Mount and Jesus' powerful call to bear the cross and live under the yoke.

First we will study Jesus' description of the believer's beatitude-based character, salt and light impact, and life-shaping dependence on the Word of God. From there we will examine the difference between heart righteousness and self-righteousness. In the Sermon on the Mount, Jesus reveals the visible righteousness characteristic of the believer's life; the down-to-earth, practical faithfulness of love instead of anger, purity instead of lust, fidelity instead of infidelity, reconciliation instead of retaliation.

Jesus then leads us deeper into discipleship by describing the spiritual disciplines of hidden righteousness. He shows us the true nature of soul-satisfying prayer, heartfelt giving, and God-focused fasting. Jesus offers penetrating insight into our priorities and passions, our work and our worries.

In the process, Jesus shows us how we can experience the reality of the easy yoke and discover the rhythm of life and rest of soul that Jesus promises.

In the Sermon on the Mount, Jesus redefines the meaning of easy. His easy yoke is neither cheap nor convenient. The surprising promise of the easy yoke was meant to free us from a self-serving, meritorious, performance-based religion. It is easy in that it frees us from the burden of self-centeredness; liberates us from the load of self-righteousness; and frees us to live in the way that God intended us to live.

$\mathscr{A}$t that time Jesus said, "I praise you, Father, Lord of heaven and earth, because you have hidden these things from the wise and learned, and revealed them to little children. Yes, Father, for this was your good pleasure.

"All things have been committed to me by my Father. No one knows the Son except the Father, and no one knows the Father except the Son and those to whom the Son chooses to reveal him.

"Come to me, all you who are weary and burdened, and I will give you rest. Take my yoke upon you and learn from me, for I am gentle and humble in heart, and you will find rest for your souls. For my yoke is easy and my burden is light."

MATTHEW 11:25-30

CHAPTER ONE

Who Stole the Easy Yoke?

A strange paradox afflicts modern life. On the one hand, we have never had it so good; on the other, we have never been so empty.

We have every time-saving convenience possible, but we have no rest. We have sophisticated, hi-tech communications, but we have no communion; many churches, but little spirituality; an abundance of lawyers, but a poverty of justice. We have an army of counselors, therapists, and psychologists trying to plug the dike, but the flood of human brokenness continues. We have an insatiable desire for intimacy, but an incapacity to commit ourselves to one another in marriage, in parenting, in friendship.

It is the best of times for recreation, the worst of times for righteousness. It is the best of times for health care, the worst of times for wholeness. It is the best of times for technology, the worst of times for truth. It is the best of times for sexual freedom, the worst of times for relational happiness. We are acutely aware of the problem of insignificance. In a land of plenty, we are famished spiritually, morally, and relationally.

For many, living has become synonymous with coping . . . surviving . . . taking one day at a time. What makes these times so hard? Are these real, honest-to-goodness hard times, or are we complainers, griping when we should be thankful?

Barbara Tuchman, in her book *A Distant Mirror,* describes Europe in the fourteenth century when Europe was decimated by the bubonic plague.[1] Would anyone who lived through the Black Death have sympathy for Americans in the 1990s? Are we like spoiled children who don't know how good we have it? Or are we experiencing a "black death" of our own—a black death of the soul?

One of the spiritual epicenters for this black death—this quaking of the soul—is southern California, where I live. This region illustrates the difference between tourist-perfect appearance and soul-denying reality. Here people live on the edge between paradise and chaos. Southern California is to the soul what Beirut and Bosnia are to politics—a war zone of the heart. It is a beautiful place to live, but a warning to the rest of the country. The nation talks about California's hard times: riots, fires, earthquakes, unemployment, the cost of living, drugs, divorce, decadence, and violence. It's becoming hard to live in southern California, whose reputation for easy living is challenged by the reality of hard times. The barber, the check-out clerk, and the auto mechanic want out. It's hard to live when the earth gives way.

But that's not the only thing giving way. Marriages and jobs, hopes and dreams are collapsing and crumbling. You fear getting AIDS in a McDonalds' bathroom. You fear the C-word— the dreaded diagnosis of cancer. You fear falling and breaking a hip, getting mugged, being alone. Your money runs out before the month does. Your children are getting divorced. Geological fault lines below and countless relational, moral, spiritual, and sexual fault lines within. It's just another day in paradise, but below the surface the pressures keep building.

Increasingly, the pressures of life spread equally from coast to coast. What does the church say to a people living on the edge in the American heartland or in the deep South? Jesus invites us to rest: "Come to me, all you who are weary and burdened, and I will give you rest. Take my yoke . . . and you will find rest for your souls. For my yoke is easy and my burden is light" (Matthew 11:28-30). Can His invitation be heard over the noise of the crowd? We know the times are hard, so what is easy about the easy yoke? What is light about Jesus' burden?

To most of us, this talk of an easy yoke sounds odd. More familiar with molecules than mules, we are likely to ask, "Does an easy yoke mean you like your eggs over-easy, soft and runny?" A yoke is a device used from ancient times to couple together two animals, especially oxen, for drawing a plow or pulling a cart. With a stretch of the imagination you might think of a bicycle built for two. For Jesus' audience, the metaphor made sense immediately. Jesus was inviting people to follow Him, step by step, into salvation, strength, and soul-rest. Leave your aloneness and emptiness, He advised, and come follow Me.

It's not easy to define easy. The word *easy* sends us off in all sorts of pleasing directions. *Easy* is synonymous with user-friendly, stress-free, laid-back. If something is easy then it is not difficult or burdensome. *Easy* means no homework, no-fault divorce, no pressure, no commitment. To be easy to get along with is a compliment. *Easy* translates into American amazingly well. It equates with no-wait convenience, instant service, and a pain-free life. *Easy* means fun. It is the cornerstone to leisure and entertainment. If the Eskimos have many words for *snow*, we have many more for *easy*. And if we rhyme ideas instead of sounds, *easy* rhymes with *America*.

Does the meaning of the easy yoke get lost in translation? We translate from the Greek word *chrestos* to the American word *easy* and something is missing. There is an intuitive sense that meaning has been lost. We jump from the usual meaning of *chrestos,* that which is good and kind, to the more familiar *easy*. Unfortunately, what makes good sense philosophically— yokes cannot be said to be moral and kind—misleads us theologically. With a linguistic sleight of hand, we shift from character to convenience. Living is reduced to a lifestyle.

In today's vernacular, that which is "easy, efficient, and

exciting" is stripped of spirituality and morality. We have taken
ethics out of the meaning of *easy*. We confuse the character-
building, soul-developing, brother-let-me-be-your servant *easy*
with the pain-free, laid-back, "everyone does what is right in
his own eyes" *easy*. Trying to make things easy, we have ended
up making things hard. *Yoke* has been written in small print
and *easy* in capital letters.

THE MISSING YOKE
The easy yoke sounds like an oxymoron. Plowing a field or
pulling a load is hard work! And nowhere does Jesus promise
soft ground for tilling or level paths for bearing the load. What
Jesus does promise is a relationship with Himself. The
demands are great but the relationship with Jesus makes the
burden light.

The yoke can be a symbol of oppression (see Isaiah 9:4,
58:6; Jeremiah 27–28) or a symbol of relationship to God (Jeremiah 2:20, Lamentations 3:27). In Matthew, Jesus used the
metaphor in a positive way to convey the importance of the
disciple relationship. To be yoked is to be related, connected,
networked with Jesus. The disciple follows Jesus' lead and
learns from Him the way an apprentice learns from a master
craftsman or the resident doctor learns from an established
physician. To be yoked to Jesus is to be mentored, directed,
guided, and equipped by the only One who can give us rest.
This is the one yoke that delivers on the promise to lighten
the load, because the burden is truly shared; Jesus meant it to
be a comforting, reassuring picture.

The easy yoke embodies the relational theology that Jesus
had in mind. The Apostle Paul had another yoke in mind,
when he wrote to the Galatians: "It is for freedom that Christ
has set us free. Stand firm, then, and do not let yourselves be
burdened again by a yoke of slavery" (5:1). Paul warned believers not to exchange the easy yoke of Jesus for the yoke of slavery. We face the same danger today.

American Christians are missing something: the yoke. In an

effort to make the Christian life easy, we end up making it hard. In our longing to lighten the load, we have removed the yoke and made life unbearable. It is the reason we are finding living so difficult, the burden so heavy, and the path so lonely. It explains why people are falling apart, rusting out, burning out, breaking up, giving up. The unyoked Christian does not know how to feel, what to think, where to go. We have given the Christian everything but the encouragement to take up the yoke. We have given people entertaining worship, support groups, exciting activities, and professional care, but we have taken away the yoke.

We have made following Jesus easy in the convenient, casual sense of the word: Worship when you feel like it; demand excellence, fun, and excitement in your church services; expect more out of your church and you'll get it. We pay more attention to a person's feelings than to his or her faith. In a variety of ways, mainline churches and market-driven churches have removed the yoke of Jesus. They have lifted it from our shoulders and apologized on behalf of Jesus for demanding too much from us. Instead of a yoke, we have been given a free pass to the next performance. Instead of sojourners, we are spectators. Instead of the Body of Christ, we are a religious audience. Yet without the yoke, life is unbearable.

In an effort to make things easy we have ended up making them hard. It is especially critical that we reexamine the meaning of Jesus' invitation and how He gave it. For this is the most important invitation we will ever receive. Many professing believers are laboring under a yoke of bondage because they have never heard Jesus' invitation of the easy yoke.

WHO CANCELED THE INVITATION?

We fail to give the invitation to the people who need it the most by assuming that the people in the pew are Christians. Jesus says directly and definitively, "Come to me." But many religious people have no history of coming to Jesus personally. They are Episcopalians, Methodists, Presbyterians, but they do not know Christ. They attend church but they don't belong to the Body of Christ. They have never experienced or responded to the personal invitation of Jesus, "Come to me."

Those of us in the mainline church suspect we might offend some people if we say a personal relationship with Jesus Christ is necessary for salvation and that it is essential for living the Christian life. But we cannot gloss over the fact that Jesus has boldly and personally said, "Come to me." He is either the way, the truth, and the life, or He is a self-appointed messianic cult figure or legendary creation of the First Church of the Deceivers. He is either fact or fiction.

Because they fear being charged with exclusivity or offending people's pride or intruding on their privacy, some believers play down the clear, compelling invitation to come to Jesus, our only hope for salvation. But this leaves people trying to live the Christian life without knowing Christ, forced to pretend they have peace and forgiveness when all they have is religious sentiment and spiritual feelings. The unconverted may be moved by the liturgy and satisfied by their religious tradition, but they do not know the wisdom and power of Christ to transform their lives. They have a form of godliness, but they don't know the power of God. Apart from the invitation, the Christian life is impossible.

Jesus' invitation makes living under the yoke easy and the burden light. To receive it and respond to Christ is our greatest blessing. To offer it to others is an honor, not a liability. What makes the yoke easy is the One who invites us to come. And as a wonderful expression of His grace and mercy, He is persistent in his invitation. C. S. Lewis's response to the invitation is a classic example of what many have experienced.

> Remember, I had always wanted, above all things, not to be "interfered with." I had wanted (mad wish) "to call my soul my own." . . . You must picture me alone . . . , night after night, feeling, whenever my mind lifted even for a second from my work, the steady, unrelenting

approach of Him whom I so earnestly desired not to meet. That which I greatly feared had at last come upon me. . . . [Finally] I gave in and admitted that God was God, and knelt and prayed: perhaps, that night, the most dejected and reluctant convert in all England. I did not then see what is now the most shining and obvious thing; the Divine humility which will accept a convert even on such terms. The Prodigal Son at least walked home on his own feet. But who can duly adore that Love which will open the high gates to a prodigal who is brought in kicking, struggling, resentful, and darting his eyes in every direction for a chance of escape? The words, "compel them to come in," have been so abused by wicked men that we shudder at them; but properly understood, they plumb the depth of the Divine mercy. The hardness of God is kinder than the softness of men, and His compulsion is our liberation.[2]

WHO TURNED THE INVITATION INTO A SALES PITCH?

If mainline churches are embarrassed about Jesus' invitation to take up His yoke and follow Him, market-driven churches are too casual and flippant with it. They often sell the gospel cheap, just another commodity designed to make life easy. The invitation is handled with marketing finesse and manipulated to dovetail with self-help strategies and self-esteem issues. Instead of the mainline proclivity for an abstract Christ who is lord of diversity and inclusiveness, Jesus is presented as a pop-psychologist who helps people feel good about themselves. But "easy believism" is not what Jesus meant by the easy yoke. Bonhoeffer wrote:

Cheap grace is grace without discipleship, grace without the cross, grace without Jesus Christ, living and incarnate. . . . It is costly because it costs a person his life, and it is grace because it gives a person the only true life. It is costly because it condemns sin, and grace because it justifies the sinner. Above all, it is costly because it cost God the life of his Son: "You were bought at a price," and what has cost God much cannot be cheap for us. Above all, it is grace because God did not reckon his Son too dear a price to pay for our life, but delivered him up for us. Costly grace is the Incarnation of God.[3]

When we respond to the invitation of Jesus instead of falling for the marketing pitch of cheap grace, our lives are transformed from the inside out and from top to bottom. The Word of Christ changes the way we measure success, determine priorities, parent our children, and pray. We echo the words of Paul, "I consider everything a loss compared to the surpassing greatness of knowing Christ Jesus my Lord, for whose sake I have lost all things" (Philippians 3:8).

Coming to Christ should mean what it meant for Paul, leaving his former objects of trust and confidence: pride of race, religious merit, family privilege, ideological commitments, and his passion for a religious cause. The means of salvation is no longer in our hands, and we know it. We give up all recourse to self-salvation. We gratefully turn off the old-life support system in order to enjoy new life in Christ. With Paul we say, "I consider them rubbish, that I may gain Christ and be found in him, not having a righteousness of my own that comes from the law, but that which is through faith in Christ" (3:8-9). Paul's famous line, "For to me, to live is Christ and to die is gain" (1:21), expressed the meaning of accepting the invitation.

Undeniably, there is a radical quality to the easy yoke. When we come to Jesus we are invited to lay aside our pretentiousness and self-confidence and accept the fact of our weakness. We admit we are "harassed and helpless, like sheep without a shepherd." We are sinners in need of God's grace and forgiveness. We have learned how hard it is to depend upon ourselves. Before Jesus, we can finally admit it, because Jesus slays the fatted calf of self-esteem.

Former coach at North Carolina State and ABC sports announcer, Jim Valvano, died last year from cancer, but not before expressing the futility of his life. His interview with *Sports Illustrated*, entitled "As Time Runs Out," was one of the most moving expressions of human helplessness I have read.[4] He fought the disease the way he coached basketball, with a passionate competitiveness, but he wasn't able to pull out a win before the buzzer sounded. "I'm helpless! I make no decisions! I have no control! I'm totally at the mercy of the disease and the treatment! I'm not a dad! I'm not a husband! I'm a freak! I can't do anything! I just lie there and they stick needles into this lump in my chest and pour poison in my body, and I don't believe in it. I'm a freak!"

When his team won the NCAA championship, his players asked their wildly ecstatic coach, "Why is winning so important to you?"

"Because the final score defines you," he said. "You lose; ergo, you're a loser. You win; ergo, you're a winner."

But as Valvano learned, the "survival of the fittest" philosophy of life means we are all losers eventually. "The triviality of it just clobbers me. You get this sick and you say to yourself, 'Sports means nothing,' and that feels terrible. God, I devoted my whole life to it. People think a sports background helps you fight death. Are you kidding? Athletes and coaches are taught that they're special. You're nobody when you're a cancer patient. You're nobody."

Life did not turn out the way Jim Valvano expected. "I figured I'd have twenty years in the big-time, who knows, maybe win three national titles, then pack it in at fifty-three or fifty-four, walk into the house one day, put on a sweater and announce: 'Here I am! Ozzie Nelson's here! I'm yours!' I always saw myself as becoming the all-time-great grandfather. Leave the kids with me? No problem . . . I was going to make it up to them, all the time I'd been away." His eyes welled up with tears. "God . . . it sounds so silly now. . . . But I didn't feel guilt about it then. My thinking always was, I would make a life so exciting that my wife and kids would be thrilled just to be a part of it. . . . But it went on and on, that insatiable desire to conquer the world. I was an arrogant son of a. . . . But it wasn't just arrogance. . . ."

Our unwillingness to admit our weakness and sin compounds our dilemma. We expect a final quarter "comeback," when against the odds we rise above our circumstances, above the crowd, and declare victory. We want an NFL come-from-behind win; what we need is a prodigal son homecoming. We want the envy of the crowd; we need the embrace of our heavenly Father. The yoke is easy precisely because Jesus knows who we are in our weakness and sinfulness. Coming to Jesus and taking up His yoke removes the pressure of pretense.

We remove the easy yoke when we separate coming to Christ from following Christ. Jesus insists we remove divided loyalties and captivating idols: "If anyone comes to me and does not hate his father and mother, his wife and children, his brothers and sisters—yes, even his own life—he cannot be my disciple" (Luke 14:26). If we cling to our lives selfishly or materialistically, we are trying to get out from under the easy yoke.

Jesus told the rich young ruler, "Sell everything you have and give to the poor, and you will have treasure in heaven" (18:22). Anything—anything at all—that becomes an excuse for throwing off the yoke makes the Christian life unbearable. "Any of you who does not give up everything he has cannot be my disciple" (14:33).

No follower of Christ will deny that there is a cost to taking up the easy yoke. It is not convenient or comfortable. No true disciple has ever said it is a casual, carefree yoke. But compare the cost of living in Christ to the cost of living apart from Christ. This thought prompted the Danish Christian philosopher, Sören Kierkegaard, to write, "It costs a man just as much or even more to go to hell than to come to heaven. Narrow, exceedingly narrow is the way to perdition!"[5] This is one invitation we cannot afford to turn down; one strategy for living that surpasses every other; one relationship that enables us to live in and beyond the hard times. If it works in the spiritual mess and muddle of southern California, it will work where you live.

Jesus offers His invitation on His terms, because these are the only terms that will work. Any other arrangement places us under a yoke of bondage. In the following chapters we'll explore what it means to accept the invitation of Jesus, to lay aside our self-reliance and self-righteousness, and to experience life under the easy yoke.

In the Sermon on the Mount Jesus shows us what life looks like when it is yoked to Him. The secret of easy-yoke happiness may be surprising, but it is not a mystery. Like the relationship between good friends or the partnership in a great marriage, the commitment is challenging but not condemning, comforting but not controlling. Our bond with Christ makes the difference between blessing and bondage.

> Grace is costly because it compels a person to submit
> to the yoke of Christ and follow him; it is grace because
> Jesus says: "My yoke is easy and my burden is light."[6]

*A*bruptly Jesus broke into prayer: "Thank you, Father, Lord of heaven and earth. You've concealed your ways from sophisticates and know-it-alls, but spelled them out clearly to ordinary people. Yes, Father, that's the way you like to work."

Jesus resumed talking to the people, but now tenderly. "The Father has given me all these things to do and say. This is a unique Father-Son operation, coming out of Father and Son intimacies and knowledge. No one knows the Son the way the Father does, nor the Father the way the Son does. But I'm not keeping it to myself; I'm ready to go over it line by line with anyone willing to listen.

"Are you tired?" Jesus asks. "Worn out? Burned out on religion? Come to me. Get away with me and you'll recover your life. I'll show you how to take a real rest. Walk with me and work with me—watch how I do it. Learn the unforced rhythms of grace. I won't lay anything heavy or ill-fitting on you. Keep company with me and you'll learn to live freely and lightly."

MATTHEW 11:25-30, *THE MESSAGE*

Now when he saw the crowds, he went up on a mountainside and sat down. His disciples came to him, and he began to teach them, saying:

"Blessed are the poor in spirit,
for theirs is the kingdom of heaven.
Blessed are those who mourn,
for they will be comforted.
Blessed are the meek,
for they will inherit the earth.
Blessed are those who hunger and thirst for righteousness,
for they will be filled.
Blessed are the merciful,
for they will be shown mercy.
Blessed are the pure in heart,
for they will see God.
Blessed are the peacemakers,
for they will be called sons of God.
Blessed are those who are persecuted because of righteousness,
for theirs is the kingdom of heaven.

"Blessed are you when people insult you, persecute you and falsely say all kinds of evil against you because of me. Rejoice and be glad, because great is your reward in heaven, for in the same way they persecuted the prophets who were before you."

MATTHEW 5:1-12

CHAPTER TWO

Happiness Is Serious Business

It's amusing to watch a young mother or father calling their one-year-old to "come." The child hears and understands. You can see comprehension in the child's eyes. Then the youngster turns and skedaddles off in the opposite direction as fast as his little legs will go. It's not that he doesn't recognize the voice of authority or perceive the intent of the command or make out the words. The word *come* is one of the first words in a child's vocabulary, along with *no, stop,* and *mommy.* The child is simply testing his will against his parent's.

Jesus' invitation, "Come to me," is no more complicated. The spiritual direction He gives is simple. We recognize His authority and we understand His invitation. Pride, however, turns the simple invitation into a complex conflict of wills, soliciting from us a range of excuses. We are strongly tempted to run off in the opposite direction. Our selfish human tendency toward personal autonomy and self-centeredness insists on being the final arbiter of truth.

Only humility of heart and mind can help us accept Jesus' invitation as the call of God. Jesus described this openness to God as a childlike trust and acceptance. "I tell you the truth, unless you change and become like little children, you will never enter the kingdom of heaven" (Matthew 18:3). Elaborate adult defenses can be penetrated by the love of God; God's revelation cuts through the sophistry and selfish pride. We cannot even take credit for our response. God is there, going before, revealing, convicting, and comforting. "I praise you, Father, Lord of heaven and earth, because you have hidden these things from the wise and learned, and revealed them to little children" (Matthew 11:25).

Increasingly, professing Christians question whether Jesus' teaching is authoritative and relevant for today. Mainline churches recognize the Lordship of Christ as a glorious abstraction sanctifying widely disparate views on everything from salvation to sexuality. Market-driven churches tend to present Jesus as a friend who consoles, supports, encourages, and affirms but never rebukes, condemns, or commands. It is precisely this distancing from the teaching of Jesus that removes the yoke and creates an impossible burden. We are offered the Christian life artificially, without the strategy of Jesus to live it authentically.

Jesus, however, linked His invitation to His teaching. His personal self-claim is so integrated with everything He taught that to separate the two is to destroy them both. He made His personal identity the central issue of His teaching. His entirely original stance toward the Law and His claim to absolute authority make it impossible to differentiate the teacher's identity from His instruction. Wisdom cannot be abstracted from His person, since it is embodied and empowered through Him. Jesus is certainly more than a great teacher, but He is not less than a teacher. The same grace that enables us to respond to the invitation enables us to receive and obey the instruction.

A GOSPEL OF OBEDIENCE

The Sermon on the Mount is perfect "follow-up" instruction describing what it means to follow Jesus. It is a concise, yet comprehensive description of Jesus' strategy for living. We cannot come to this teaching and expect to respond effectively and faithfully without first coming to Jesus, nor can we expect to come to Jesus without taking His teaching seriously. The invitation, "Come to me" and the instruction, "Take my yoke upon you and learn from me," go hand in hand (Matthew 11:28-30). Our evangelism does not always make this clear. Jesus combines the gospel of grace with the gospel of obedience. To know Christ is to become like Jesus. If we accept His invitation, we commence a lifelong journey in yoked fellowship with Jesus. By God's grace we have chosen the road less traveled, but it is the only road worth traveling. We listen intently to the One who will guide us along that path of wisdom and shalom.

Jesus begins the Sermon on the Mount seated. In contrast, we begin everything with a flurry of activity. We like to do things fast and furiously. We've been taught to pay attention to special effects and amplified sounds. The most expensive modern art form is the thirty-second commercial—a collage of mini-second images thrown against your brain for the sake of impact, not thought. But Jesus sits down and teaches us eye to eye, heart to heart, mind to mind. Against every high-strung emotion and attention-deficit disorder impulse, He calls us to sit down and listen.

The way Jesus wants to teach us is different from many modern preachers. Biblical preaching calls for a clear presentation of the whole counsel of God in a style that commends personal consideration, serious thought, and practical application. It's difficult to measure Jesus' charisma in the Sermon on the Mount or to imagine many today finding Him an attractive speaker. There are no amusing anecdotes, heart-tugging human interest stories, or clever one-liners. What we can imagine, however, is His soul-searching, penetrating presentation of truth that has the quality of being personal, practical, and profound all at the same time.

Actor Steve Martin's caricature of an evangelist in *Leap of Faith* is both entertaining and sobering. He parodies contemporary preaching so effectively that his technique invites review in seminary homiletics classes. It's sobering to think how large

Steve Martin's church would be if he gave up acting for preaching. Today's style is a fast-paced mix of dramatic gestures, rapid-fire verbal impact, and logic designed to move the heart without necessarily bothering the brain. Such a style divorces the public performer from the backstage private person and creates, as it did in Steve Martin's movie, a disdain for the religious audience as a bunch of "suckers."

Sadly there are two broad categories of churchgoers: those who expect to be bored and those who expect to be entertained. One group receives a predictable, pedantic sermonette and the other an entertaining, felt–need-focused, self-promoting performance. But when we carefully listen to Jesus in the Sermon on the Mount, we are neither bored nor entertained. Religious platitudes and performances are set aside and the soul-developing, life-transforming gospel is offered person to person.

Since nothing about Jesus' style makes trivial either the truth or the disciple, it is important that we not use Jesus to sell cheap grace. Neil Postman imagines a television commercial in the not too distant future depicting a Middle Eastern oasis, with palm trees swaying and music playing in the background. A bearded man in a long flowing robe, reminiscent of the portrait of Jesus, holds up a bottle of Chardonnay and says, "This is what I had in mind when I turned the water to wine."[1] Postman observes that this is not so much blasphemy as trivilization. When Jesus is used by a marketer to sell a product, that which is sacred is profaned, and truth is made trivial.

Postman's illustration of the "Jesus commercial" is futuristic. To date, Madison Avenue has refrained from pitching products with Jesus as their spokesperson. But that has not stopped the church from abusing the image of Christ. Instead of emptying Jesus of His specific content and teaching, the church needs to sit down and listen to what Jesus would say to us today. "In the last resort," writes Dietrich Bonhoeffer, "what we want to know is not, what would this or that person or this or that church have of us, but what Jesus Christ himself wants from us."[2] Dallas Willard writes: "The secret of the easy yoke is simple, actually. It is the intelligent, informed, unyielding resolve to live as Jesus lived in all aspects of life."[3] To do that we need to listen to Jesus carefully, patiently, thoughtfully. This may be a new experience for some who have been Christians for a long time. But Jesus does everything He can to perk up our ears and get us to listen.

AMERICA'S BEATITUDES

Jesus begins the Sermon on the Mount by talking about happiness. This is a great starting point, especially for Americans. Never have people taken the pursuit of happiness more seriously than we do today. Everywhere, people are working at it. Stroll along the harbor boardwalk and observe the megabucks invested in happiness, or sit in the coffee shop at the *Ritz Carlton* in Aspen and see how much effort and energy go into making happiness. Apparently our passion for pleasure knows no bounds. We have become the sports and entertainment capital of the world. Happiness sets the priorities. How many teachers does it take to earn the equivalent pay of the Dallas Cowboys' quarterback?

American happiness is a collage of bright images: sexy women, sexy men, sexy cars, sexy beer, sexy sports. Happiness has a lot of sex appeal. Happiness can be bought, earned, mortgaged, or credited to your account. It is a state of feeling: feeling important, feeling excited, feeling successful, feeling free, feeling good about yourself, feeling loved. When it comes to happiness American-style, the art of living is knowing where to live, not how to live. It is a quest for success, style, sex, and self-fulfillment. How would you fill in the blank, "Happiness is . . ."? The bottom line for America's philosophy of happiness can be summarized in these axioms: "You only go around once in life; you've got to grab all the gusto you can," "Think happy thoughts," "Look out for number one," "Don't worry, be happy!"

The caption under the sign at Disneyland reads, "The Happiest Place on Earth." Throughout my visit there I had cause to question the motto as I observed humanity. I marveled at how patient people were standing in long lines for up to an hour and a half for a six-minute ride. I wondered if people would be that patient waiting for a doctor or seeking after truth.

The problem with Disneyland is not long lines, interesting rides, and clever special effects. The problem is that its philosophy of happiness has escaped Anaheim and spread throughout America. There is a whole generation of Peter Pans who have never grown up, who think they are in never-never land. We have become a nation that reads the Declaration of Independence with a Disneyland understanding of happiness. We have an inalienable right to pursue pleasure with all our hearts, minds, souls, and strength. Hedonism—pleasure at all costs, in all its forms, has become an American tradition. America's Beatitudes are as popular as they are pleasure seeking. How would we articulate them?

Blessed are those who believe in themselves, for they will be successful.

Blessed are those who are in touch with their feelings, for they will feel good.

Blessed are the self-assertive, for they will get ahead.

Blessed are the open-minded, for they will be respected.

Blessed are the tolerant, for they will be accepted.

Blessed are those who are in good shape, for they will be envied.

Blessed are the sensitive and fun-loving, for they will find intimacy.

Blessed are the popular, for theirs is the world.

The pursuit of happiness guided by Jesus and the pursuit of happiness inspired by our culture are two radically different journeys. But today's church often blurs this sharp contrast. The church is subtle and sophisticated in adapting to the cultural pursuit of happiness and making it sound spiritual. It would not be too difficult for "seekers" to conclude that the church was designed to meet their consumer-oriented felt needs rather than their fundamental spiritual needs for reconciliation with God.

The blatant, self-indulgent quest for personal pleasure in the culture becomes transposed in the market-driven church into a new key, but the tune remains the same. The church indulges the baby boomers' agenda for togetherness without commitment, for self-esteem without sacrifice. Sermons are framed in such a way that the listener focuses on self. The Bible's merit is utilitarian, serving as a practical manual for financial success, marital intimacy, effective parenting, and emotional health. But christianized self-help strategies are not what Jesus had in mind when He described the path to happiness.

A DRAMATIC CONTRAST

Jesus' alternative route to happiness begins with a declaration of dependence, not independence. The first step under the yoke is an admission of overwhelming need, and the first feeling under the yoke is overwhelming sorrow. Jesus reveals a dramatic new twist to the ancient search for happiness. The key to happiness begins with poverty, not pride; sorrow, not fun.

Jesus repeats the word *blessed* nine times. That much repetition is designed to make a point. God's blessing is received through an amazing reversal of human values. Everything we have been sold about the "easy life" is wrong: put yourself first and you will come in last, give yourself to sexual pleasure and you rape your soul, strive to be envied and you will feel lonely. Hunger and thirst for the good life and you will come away empty. "Jesus told of a blessedness not discernible in the ordinary course of things," writes Don McCullough.[4] It is hidden in the will and Word of God. You will not find it talked about in the press or on campus or in the office.

The contrast between happiness as it is popularly perceived and happiness described by Jesus in the Beatitudes could not be drawn any sharper. This contrast is apparent in the Greek translation of the New Testament. From Aristotle onward, classical Greek understood *makarios,* the word we translate as "happy" or "blessed," as a description of privilege experienced by those who were sufficiently well-off, socially and materially, to enable them to live above the worries and cares of the less fortunate.[5] This is not what Jesus had in mind when He used the word, even though His original audience and certainly His later readers would have understood the radical twist and revolutionary meaning He was giving to happiness.

Jesus drew on the Jewish roots of the word *blessed,* which meant "to find the right path." Earl Palmer writes,

> The Hebrew word for *blessed* is *ashr.* Proverbs 3:13,17 says, "Blessed is the man who finds wisdom. . . . Her ways are pleasant ways, and all her paths are peace." *Ashr* in Proverbs means to find the right path. If you are surrounded by many confusing ways and find the right way to go, then you are happy. This Old Testament idea of happiness has to do with orientation, perspective, the discovery of what is meaningful in the midst of shallow, superficial options.[6]

Jesus' theory of happiness can be summed up in the Beatitudes as eight fundamental emotional attitudes, eight convictions of the soul, eight character qualities of the inner person. Jesus paints a portrait of His followers from the inside out. He begins with their hearts and offers a glimpse of their character. He describes who they are before He details what they do. His approach sweeps aside the techniques and formulas for spiritual success and begins with the soul.

In the movie *Dead Poet's Society*, John Keating, played by Robin Williams, is an English teacher at an Ivy League boys' school. He begins his class in poetry by having his students turn to the introduction in their textbook on poetry. While one of the students reads aloud the pedantic prose of James Evans Pritchard, Ph.D., describing how they should rank poetry, Keating plots Pritchard's rating technique on the board. The students assume this is a typical, boring introduction to another academic subject, when Keating turns from the diagram on the board and says plainly, "Excrement. That's what I think of James Evans Pritchard, Ph.D.'s, introduction to poetry. We are not laying pipe. We are understanding poetry. I want you to rip it out, and while you are at it, rip out the whole introduction. Rip it out!" Slowly, as their shocked incredulity gives way to awareness, the students begin ripping the pages from their hardback volume of poetry. "This is a battle, a war," Keating declares, "and the casualties could be your hearts and souls. Armies of academics going forth, measuring poetry. But this will not happen in my class. You will learn to savor words and language."

In the same way, the Beatitudes rip out the boring, abstract introduction to religious education and reveal the heart and soul of following Jesus. Jesus does not allow religion to get in the way of life, nor pride to get in the way of repentance.

Jesus did not begin with a preface of religious platitudes to be intoned piously for the benefit of a religious culture. Instead He began with a down-to-earth character sketch of spiritual maturity and authentic discipleship. While all the Beatitudes address the believer's character and reflect the true colors of the disciple, the scope of this book limits us to an in-depth look at only three. However, references to all the Beatitudes will be made throughout, as they have a primary contribution to every aspect of the Sermon on the Mount. For the purposes of this book, we are balancing a close look at three beatitudes with a comprehensive look at the Sermon on the Mount.

THE FIRST STEP TO DISCIPLESHIP

John Calvin defined the first beatitude succinctly: "He only who is reduced to nothing in himself, and relies on the mercy of God, is poor in spirit." Jesus drew not only on the Hebrew meaning of *blessing,* but the Old Testament understanding of the poor.

The psalms express what it means to be poor in spirit.

> This poor man called, and the LORD heard him;
>> he saved him out of all his troubles. (Psalm 34:6)

> The sacrifices of God are a broken spirit;
>> a broken and contrite heart, O God, you will not
>>> despise. (Psalm 51:17)

Isaiah's experience captures the essence of spiritual poverty:

> Woe to me! I am ruined!
> For I am a man of unclean lips,
>> and I live among a people of unclean lips,
>> and my eyes have seen the King, the LORD Almighty.
>>> (Isaiah 6:5)

"This is what the Lord says," declares Jeremiah:

> Let not the wise man boast of his wisdom or the strong man boast of his strength or the rich man boast of his riches, but let him who boasts boast about this: that he understands and knows me, that I am the LORD, who exercises kindness, justice and righteousness on earth, for in these I delight. (Jeremiah 9:23-24)

These famous lines from Chronicles sum up the starting point for the pursuit of happiness,

> "If my people, who are called by my name, will humble themselves and pray and seek my face and turn from their

wicked ways, then will I hear from heaven and will forgive their sin and will heal their land." (2 Chronicles 7:14)

The poor acknowledge their desperate need for God and their inability to merit salvation. Jesus illustrates what He means by being poor in spirit:

> Blessed is the prodigal son, who finally comes to his senses and makes the long journey home, rehearsing in his heart his painful confession, "Father, I have sinned against heaven and against you. I am no longer worthy to be called your son."
> Blessed is the repentant tax collector, who humbles himself and prays, "God, have mercy on me, a sinner."
> Blessed is Simon Peter, who fell at the feet of Jesus and said, "Go away from me, Lord; I am a sinful man."
> Blessed is the woman caught in adultery, who is compelled to turn to Jesus as her last hope.

As Don McCullough notes,

> Rembrandt's great painting of the woman caught in adultery conveys the essence of this first beatitude. The artist's use of light, as in many of his works, reveals the truth of the gospel. All light flows from Christ, the tallest figure on the canvas. The men near him, upright in self-righteousness and judgmental attitudes, stand in shadows. The sinful woman is lowest of all; she alone kneels with head bowed, poor in spirit. But the light of Christ bathes her, surrounds her with splendor. She receives grace through humility. Hers is the kingdom of heaven.[7]

Chuck Colson, noted author and founder of Prison Fellowship Ministry, was in a southeastern city to speak at the governor's prayer breakfast. A prominent business leader invited him to attend their study-luncheon. Nineteen men in all, dressed in dark suits and conservative ties, filled a large conference room, beautifully paneled on one side with rosewood and the other side with plate glass windows offering a breathtaking view of the city that these men ran and owned. Somewhere in his talk he referred to our sinful nature. Actually, "total depravity" was the term he used. A few individuals shifted uncomfortably in their leather chairs. When he finished, the first question Colson was asked was on sin.

"You don't really believe we are sinners, do you? I mean, you're too sophisticated to be one of those hellfire-and-brimstone fellows," one older gentleman said, eyeing Colson's dark-blue pinstripe suit, which was just like his. "Intelligent people don't go for that back-country preacher stuff," he added.

"Yes, sir," Colson replied. "I believe we are desperately sinful. What's inside of each of us is really pretty ugly. In fact, we deserve hell and would get it but for the sacrifice of Christ for our sins."

The host looked distressed by now. "Well, I don't know about that," he said. "I'm a good person and have been all my life. I go to church, and I get exhausted spending all my time doing good works." The room seemed particularly quiet, and nineteen pairs of eyes were trained on Colson.

"If you believe that, Mr. Abercrombie—and I hate to say this, for you certainly won't invite me back—you are, for all of your good works, further away from the kingdom than the people I work with in prison who are aware of their own sins . . . ." Someone at the other end of the table coughed . . . another rattled his coffee cup . . . Mr. Abercrombie's face flushed red. "In fact, gentlemen," Colson added, "if you think about it, we are all really more like Adolf Hitler than Jesus Christ."

When the lunch ended and Colson was preparing to leave, Mr. Abercrombie took his arm. "Didn't you say you wanted to make a phone call when we finished?" Colson realized he wanted to get him alone. . . . Abercrombie led Colson down the corridor to an empty office. As soon as they were inside, he said bluntly, "I don't have what you have." Colson replied, "I know, but you can. God is touching your heart right now."

"No, no," he took a step back. "Maybe sometime." Colson pressed a bit more, however, and moments later they were both on their knees. Mr. Abercrombie asked forgiveness for his sins and turned his life over to Christ.[8]

To be poor in spirit is to declare spiritual bankruptcy before God. It is to realize for oneself, what C. S. Lewis discovered about himself, "For the first time I examined myself with a seriously practical purpose. And there I found what appalled me; a zoo of lusts, a bedlam of ambitions, a nursery of fears, a harem of fondled hatreds. My name was legion."[9]

There is an inherent humanness about admitting our sinfulness and dependence upon God. What could be more human than honestly to confess our need? To admit otherwise is to pursue happiness through means that will never satisfy. J. I. Packer observes: "It is supremely ironic that, after two millennia of Christian culture, the West should now be plunging back into a self-defeating hedonism that is horribly similar to the barbaric pagan lifestyle of the first century, while decrying the Christian religion as basically antihuman because it does not set up pleasing oneself as life's highest value."[10]

Moving from selfish pride to spiritual poverty is an important first step on the path of discipleship, for both individual believers and for the Body of Christ, the Church. The church of Laodicea prided herself on having everything she needed: "You say, 'I am rich; I have acquired wealth and do not need a thing.'" But God's assessment was different: "You do not realize that you are wretched, pitiful, poor, blind and naked" (Revelation 3:17). The church that seeks to impress the world may succeed, but at the expense of fellowship with God. True happiness in the Body of Christ is to share the experience and the promise of this first beatitude.

God promises a Kingdom to those who overcome the American pursuit of happiness and the pleasure principles of the world. Those who have ears to hear, let them hear. To those who overcome their pride and confess their sin, Jesus promises a seat on His throne. "I will give the right to sit with me on my throne, just as I overcame and sat down with my Father on his throne" (Revelation 3:21).

The blessing of the first beatitude and the motivation for the believers in Laodicea is the Kingdom of God. Jesus confers on those who have declared spiritual bankruptcy the Kingdom of God. Only Jesus can bridge the gap from the state of our soul to the hope of eternity. "Congratulations to the poor in spirit! They are humbly open to God's control (the kingdom), and thus will be happy in this life and the next."[11]

Many Americans are unimpressed with the promise of the Kingdom of God. They have never thought about it. It is a foreign concept. When Jesus says, "Blessed are the poor in spirit, for theirs is the Kingdom of God," He might as well be speaking Swahili. Every nuance of the first beatitude requires translation. It is not immediately apparent what Jesus has in mind when He blesses the poor in spirit. Nor do many have a clue or care what is involved in the rule of God. Free tickets to the Magic Kingdom may mean more than the promise of the Kingdom of God.

෨

What does it mean to accept the invitation of Jesus, "Take my yoke upon you and learn from me, . . . for my yoke is easy and my burden is light"? What is involved in bearing this easy yoke? What is in it for us? God's truth does not always conform to our first impressions. The Beatitudes immediately challenge our assumptions and cause us to re-examine our premature conclusions about the Christian life. The character-defining work of the Beatitudes is seen throughout the portrait of the Sermon on the Mount, as if the Beatitudes are the primary colors from which everything else is painted.

*W*hen Jesus saw his ministry drawing huge crowds, he climbed a hill-side. Those who were apprenticed to him, the committed, climbed with him. Arriving at a quiet place, he sat down and taught his climbing companions. This is what he said:

"You're blessed when you're at the end of your rope. With less of you there is more of God and his rule.

"You're blessed when you feel you've lost what is most dear to you. Only then can you be embraced by the One most dear to you.

"You're blessed when you're content with just who you are—no more, no less. That's the moment you find yourselves proud owners of everything that can't be bought.

"You're blessed when you've worked up a good appetite for God. He's food and drink in the best meal you'll ever eat.

"You're blessed when you care. At the moment of being 'care-full,' you find yourselves cared for.

"You're blessed when you get your inside world—your mind and heart—put right. Then you can see God in the outside world.

"You're blessed when you can show people how to cooperate instead of compete or fight. That's when you discover who you really are, and your place in God's family.

"You're blessed when your commitment to God provokes persecution. The persecution drives you even deeper into God's kingdom.

"Not only that—count yourselves blessed every time people put you down or throw you out or speak lies about you to discredit me. What it means is that the truth is too close for comfort and they are uncomfortable. You can be glad when that happens—give a cheer, even!—for though they don't like it, *I* do! And all heaven applauds. And know that you are in good company. My prophets and witnesses have always gotten into this kind of trouble."

MATTHEW 5:1-12, *THE MESSAGE*

. . . .

"*Blessed* are those who mourn, for they will be comforted."

Matthew 5:4

CHAPTER THREE

From Blame to Blessing

The first beatitude can easily fall on deaf ears, but the second beatitude, "Blessed are those who mourn, for they will be comforted," leaves a different impression. It appears to be the easiest beatitude to understand and the most natural to fulfill, because we all feel like mourning from time to time and we all need some tender, loving care.

Most of us don't need instruction on mourning. It just happens, it's part of living. Everyone knows someone dying of cancer, some person out of work, some marriage breaking up, some family in crisis, some African nation starving, some friend fighting depression. To mourn is to grieve, to lament, to be filled with sorrow. It is not something we schedule or encourage one another to do. In some parts of the world professional mourners are employed to increase the spectacle of bereavement, but for the most part, we mourn without any help from others.

We think of mourning more as a response to tragic circumstances than a disciplined state of being. Mourning as a spiritual discipline? But is this what Jesus had in mind? The second beatitude is either a thought for a Hallmark sympathy card or a radical new twist to grief. If finding the path of blessing means being poor in spirit, then staying on that path requires a new kind of sorrow. According to Jesus, this kind of mourning does not come naturally. We don't mourn because of our circumstances; we mourn because of our condition.

THE PROBLEM WITH BLAME

Just as there are many false paths to happiness, there are many false expressions of sorrow. In the last chapter we saw how pride stands in the way of following the Lord Jesus. Selfish pride is to spiritual poverty what self-pity is to mourning. Once again the strategy of Jesus for living turns everything inside out, upside-down. For the grief we are meant to feel deeply and personally is not the nastiness of the world with all of its evil and injustices, but our very own guilt.

It is not the world that has wronged us, but we who have wronged the world. It is not only boasting, but blaming that prevents people from coming to God. Complaining is not synonymous with mourning, just as identifying the speck in our brother's eye is not the same thing as removing the beam in our own eye.

To mourn is to grieve the loss of our innocence, to lament our unrighteousness, to be filled with sorrow because of our sinfulness. The tragedy of this world is not primarily social and political, it's personal. It begins with me. British author G. K. Chesterton was asked to write a magazine article on the subject, "What's wrong with the universe?" He responded to the editor's request with two words, "I am."

We have two primary recourses for avoiding this truth: pleasure and pity. The current philosophy "Eat, drink, and be merry for tomorrow we die" has a strong following, but gaining momentum is a don't-blame-me permissiveness. Comedian Flip Wilson drew laughs with his contorted facial expressions and his famous one-liner, "The Devil made me do it!" But in a society of victims, no one is laughing; everyone is blaming. "I am a sinner" has evolved into, "I am a victim."

"The ethos of victimization" writes Charles Sykes, "has an endless capacity not only for exculpating one's self from blame, washing away responsibility in a torrent of explanation—racism, sexism, rotten parents, addiction, and illness—but also projecting guilt onto others."[1] Sykes argues that America has become a nation of finger pointers, adept at blaming one's ills on society, dysfunctional families, poor education, government bureaucracy, racism, sexism, or psychological maladjustment. In short, blaming everybody and everything but one's self. Today's therapeutic culture has succeeded in raising people's expectations and sensitivities.

If there was a single war cry, Sykes suggests, it might be "I deserve . . . ." As one writer declared, "I deserve love. I deserve to be trusted. I deserve freedom. I deserve friendship. I deserve respect. I deserve sexual pleasure. I deserve happiness."[2] We come at life with a we-expect-more-of-everything attitude, and when we are disappointed we blame a host of reasons. "If only," becomes a self-justifying refrain. If only I had more money. If only I had more competent parents. If only I had a few breaks. If only I was more intelligent, more attractive, more successful. If there is any thought of God, it is tinged with disappointment. "How could God let me down? Doesn't God care?" When things go wrong, the most commonly asked question is, "Why me?"

There is certainly a place for telling God how we feel and praying out our pain and disappointment. Psalms of lament bear powerful testimony to the importance of directing our emotional intensity toward God. God welcomes an honest heart willing to bare itself in order to strengthen the spirit. Turning to God in prayer when our hearts are broken requires conviction and courage. It is an act of faith and an expression of trust. We believe God shares our anger over sin and enters into our pain. But prayers of lament and confession are different from ego-inflated complaints that hold God in contempt. It is the difference between the spoiled Israelites, grumbling and complaining, and the soul-searing integrity of Job. It is the difference between a whining child ready to throw a tantrum, and a hurting child in need of comfort.

Blame desensitizes people to the root problem of evil. By universalizing victimhood, our society has not gained a clearer, truer understanding of personal and social evil. It is getting harder to mourn for our personal sins, because society offers us so many excuses. Expert witnesses are ready with explanation and defense in hand. For many there is no such thing as a personal moral choice for which we are responsible. More and more people feel they are the product of their DNA, parenting, schooling, and economics.

You may recall the tragedy in New York's Central Park when thirty boys, most under the age of sixteen, went "wilding." They raped and battered a twenty-eight-year-old jogger. What caused this gang to viciously, unmercifully attack this woman? The experts knew why: alienation, peer pressure, inequality, status anxieties, television, and advertising. Apparently the jogger was a target because she represented a level of social standing to which these boys had no hope of achieving. The fact that a homeless person was also one of the gang's eight victims on the night they went wilding was a minor discrepancy in the conclusion. In spite of this learned analysis, one of the boys blurted out the reason why they did it: "It was something to do. It was fun."

"The ambition of the modern mind," writes George Will, "is to spare itself a chilling sight, that of the cold blank stare of personal evil. The modern program is squeamishness dressed up as sophistication. Its aim is to make the reality of evil disappear behind a rhetorical gauze of learned garbage."[3]

The much publicized Erik and Lyle Menendez trials in 1993 nearly enshrine the no-fault defense strategy. With the juries hopelessly deadlocked, the judge ruled a mistrial, even though the defense conceded that the brothers had with premeditation killed both their parents with a shotgun at pointblank range as they were eating ice cream and watching television. The defense argued that the young men suffered such terrible abuse from their father that they could no longer think rationally. They killed their parents in self-defense. As one legal expert observed, the defense was able to build sympathy for the boys by months of emotional exposure. The jury entered into their emotional trauma and fear.

The prosecution, on the other hand, failed to bring the parents into the courtroom in the same emotionally identifying way. The parents, of course, are no longer available for our sympathy. Judgment is based on feelings and appearances, prompting screenwriter Paul Ciotti to say, "If the Menendez brothers aren't guilty of murder, then no one in this country is ever guilty of anything." No matter what anyone does, it's the fault of "the system." According to Ciotti, "a significant portion of the California public now believes that no one is responsible for anything."[4]

When a culture disowns moral responsibility and places the blame on someone other than the individual sinner, it becomes more and more difficult for individuals to be honest about their true spiritual condition. We see ourselves as a nation of victims, not sinners, in need of sympathy, not forgiveness. Having misdiagnosed the human condition, the prescription for healing our moral pain is ineffective.

When the bubonic plague swept through Europe killing nearly 50 percent of the population by the end of the fourteenth century, the source of the Black Death remained a mystery. "Ignorance of the cause augmented the sense of horror."[5] The deadly germ spread to humans and animals through the bite of a flea or a rat. It was further spread among humans by contact, because it infected the bloodstream, as well as by respiratory infection when it infected the lungs. The actual plague, bacillus, remained undiscovered for another five hundred years.

Concerns we take for granted today, such as sanitation, close contact, and microscopic carriers, were unknown factors in the fourteenth century. Influenced by astrology, medieval doctors blamed the disease on contaminated air caused by the movement of stars and planets. Ironically, it was popularly believed that foul odors helped prevent the disease, prompting many people to loiter around the public latrines.

If some found the cause in the stars, others found the cause closer to home. The Jews became victims of a fourteenth-century holocaust. They were accused of starting the plague by poisoning the city wells. Entire Jewish communities were exterminated in brutal massacres. Since the source of the contagious disease was unknown, medieval man became fearful and suspicious of everything from the fresh air to their Jewish neighbor. Everything was to blame but the bacteria that caused the plague.

The increased trauma and horror experienced by medieval man due to lack of basic biological knowledge is analogous to the despair and confusion experienced by modern man due to lack of basic biblical knowledge. Medieval men were ignorant of future scientific revelations necessary to fight the plague. Today we are ignorant of the ancient revelations essential to deal with evil. In an effort to cope with evil, our culture has rationalized, psychologized and politicized it. People have done everything but personalized it. Yet, in an effort to cope and make life easier by blaming others, we end up making life impossible. We refuse to acknowledge the simple fact that we are sinners.

THE FROG IN THE KETTLE

What we desperately need is to say along with the Apostle Paul, "What a wretched man I am! Who will rescue me from this body of death?" (Romans 7:24). This is what leads James to write, "Grieve, mourn and wail. Change your laughter to mourning and your joy to gloom" (James 4:9).

When our strategies of self-deception are exposed, we move from blame to blessing. But it is especially difficult for us to see the truth about ourselves. Sören Kierkegaard once suggested that becoming aware of our own sin is like trying to see our own eyeballs. King David wrote, "For in his own eyes he flatters himself too much to detect or hate his sin" (Psalm 36:2).

We are prone to overrate our good qualities and excuse our

sins. Contrary to popular opinion, most of us do not suffer from low self-esteem but from self-serving pride. We see ourselves as better than average. Psychologist David Meyers reported the findings of a college board survey of a million high school seniors. These students were asked to compare themselves to other people their age. Seventy percent rated themselves above average in leadership ability, 2 percent as below average. "In 'ability to get along with others,' 0 percent of the 829,000 students who responded rated themselves below average, 60 percent rated themselves in the top 10 percent, and 25 percent saw themselves among the top 1 percent."[6]

The self-serving bias is not limited to high school students. One survey revealed that 94 percent of a college faculty thought of themselves as better than their average colleague. We appear to have an inherent desire to build ourselves up, which makes those around us likely scapegoats if things don't go right. If most of us think we are easy to get along with, it's not too difficult to guess who will be blamed when there's conflict: the other guy!

Our built-in insensitivity to our true state is often increased by an overexposure to certain sins. We become desensitized to greed, accustomed to gossip, callous to those in need, complacent with premarital sex, indifferent to a steady diet of media violence. Like the proverbial frog in the kettle, we don't notice the steadily rising temperature.

The Los Angeles riots in the early 1990s will be remembered for the Reginald Denny beating trial. Graphic pictures of Denny being dragged from his truck remain in the collective consciousness of the American people. Defense attorney Edi Faal represented Damian Williams, who was accused of attempted murder. Faal took the most damaging evidence, which was the crucial videotape showing Williams repeatedly beating Denny, and played it over and over to the jury. Faal sought, with some success, to numb the jury to the graphic violence. "It was very powerful evidence that will not go away," Faal said. "You don't confront it halfway. You confront it all the way and use it so much that you desensitize the jurors. [If] you look at the video-tape ten or fifteen times, you become used to it."[7]

Overexposure to sin deadens the moral pain that would cause people to mourn rather than blame. Instead of leading to repentance it fosters excuses. Sin itself is no longer acknowledged, except as a quaint euphemism for illness, addiction, dysfunction, and disorder. "We played the flute for you, and you did not dance; we sang a dirge, and you did not mourn" (Matthew 11:17).

WHY SHOULD WE MOURN?
The Word of God insists that we are sinners both as a race and as individuals. We sin collectively and personally. We sin not only because we choose to, but because sin has been chosen for us.

In a culture as individualistic as ours, it does not seem fair to blame the human race because Adam sinned. Many take issue with the Apostle Paul's teaching, "Therefore, just as sin entered the world through one man, and death through sin, and in this way death came to all [people], because all sinned" (Romans 5:12). We can claim that our connection to Adam is illegitimate, but we have to admit we act just like him. We all have reason to mourn.

Ironically, modern therapy often stresses that the root of people's problems stems from a family history of dysfunctional and distorted relationships. So, if we are unable to show love or communicate honestly, we blame our parents for their lack of love and open communication. Therapists explore the confusion and conflicts of the past in order to explain and correct the problems of the present. Admittedly, there is a linkage to the past. How we were parented and our early childhood experiences *do* affect us as adults. But some people go too far with this and claim innocence for negative behavior they should be held accountable for. Rather than accept responsibility for their personal choices, they blame their parents.

Why do people reject original sin and readily accept dysfunctional family influences? Both theology and psychology claim that the past has an essential connection with human behavior in the present. The obvious reason may be that popular psychology is often used to claim our innocence and biblical theology declares our guilt. Psychology often labels people as victims, and in many cases they are; but theology calls them sinners, and in every case that is true.

We live with a spiritual, moral, and emotional history that is not of our making. To some degree, we are in the sinful image of our parents, even as our children will reflect our biological image. We are in Adam, like it or not, and our children are in us. We don't need excuses, we need help—big time! Paul echoed the prophet Isaiah when he wrote, "For just as through the disobedience of the one man the many were made sinners, so also through the obedience of the one man the many will be made righteous" (Romans 5:19). "For God so loved the world," not because we are so lovable, but because we are so needy. "God demonstrates his own love for us in this," wrote Paul: "While we were still sinners, Christ died for us" (verse 8).

We may be helped by exploring our past, but we are redeemed when we accept the mystery of Christ's atoning death on the cross. Whatever insight we could have into our past childhood experiences or dysfunctional family situations pales in significance to our understanding that God in Christ died for us to turn away the wrath of God and liberate us from the bondage of sin. All good therapy must ultimately have its roots in redemption.

What we want is affirmation and approval; what we need is deliverance. Scaled-down forms of salvation will not work. The last thing we need is to be told we are okay; that all we are suffering from is a problem of self-esteem or boredom. List all the terrible social evils: child abuse, toxic waste, gang violence, nuclear weapons, AIDS, drug addiction, teenage suicide, traffic fatalities, divorce, rape, etc. List them all and then erase them from human experience and we still have not solved our sin problem. C. S. Lewis writes,

Niceness—wholesome, integrated personality—is an excellent thing. We must try by every medical, educational, economic, and political means in our power to produce a world where as many people as possible grow up "nice"; just as we must try to produce a world where all have plenty to eat. But we must not suppose that even if we succeeded in making everyone nice we should have saved their souls. A world of nice people, content in their own niceness, looking no further, turned away from God, would be just as desperately in need of salvation as a miserable world—and even might be more difficult to save.[8]

Martin Luther used a graphic figure to depict our responsibility in the death of Christ. He said we carry around the nails of Christ's cross in our pocket. We cringe at the very thought of the crucifixion; we hardly feel responsible for spikes driven through the hands and feet of Jesus. But that is what our sins did. He "was pierced for our transgressions, he was crushed for our iniquities; the punishment that brought us peace was upon him, and by his wounds we are healed." We prefer the role of victim. It is shocking to find out that we are not the crucified, but the crucifiers.

FINDING TRUE COMFORT

I have never met anyone who mourned more painfully and in greater agony than David. The lines on his face seemed frozen and contorted in a cry of pain. His eyes, swollen and red, filled with an endless supply of tears. When he spoke, the trembling of his lips seemed to spread throughout his body. He shivered as if he were always cold. I believe David grieved as deeply as anyone could grieve. And when I visited him in prison, even his faint smile seemed to hurt.

David was in prison because he accidentally killed a mother and child on a two-lane road in Indiana. It was a Saturday afternoon and David had been drinking. He was impatient and ticked off at a motorcyclist who had passed him on a curve. He sped up to pass and lost control on the next curve. He hit the oncoming car head-on. The mother and child died instantly. It was as if in the twinkling of an eye David entered hell itself. Every evil thing he had ever done was now discharged, dumped, deposited in his despairing soul. How could a human being do what he had done? He went from an ordinary husband, okay father, average worker, to the very personification of evil. Overnight he became an object of hate in our small town. The victims' family could not have condemned David more if he had been solely responsible for the Nazi Holocaust of the Jews or singularly culpable in the crucifixion of Jesus. And who could blame them? Two white crosses marked the spot on the highway where the accident occurred. Yet throughout his ordeal David reminded me of myself; of my own sin and moral culpability. He was not alone in his need. There was a glaring obviousness about his evil, but it did not obscure my own.

The comfort we really need is not a pat on the back or an affirming nod of approval. A smile and a hug are nice and may brighten our day, but the human soul longs for a deeper comfort. The comfort promised by Jesus in the beatitude is much deeper than the approval of our friends or the solace offered by our spouse. It certainly cannot be confused with pop-psychology or public relations. His comfort is deeper and more multifaceted than the disturbing evil it promises to dispel. The psalmist comprehends the depth of this comfort when he prays,

> Praise the LORD, O my soul;
>> all my inmost being, praise his holy name.
> Praise the LORD, O my soul,
>> and forget not all his benefits—
> who forgives all your sins and heals all your diseases,
>> who redeems your life from the pit
>> and crowns you with love and compassion,
> who satisfies your desires with good things

so that your youth is renewed like the eagle's.
The LORD works righteousness
and justice for all the oppressed. (Psalm 103:1-6)

The comfort of Jesus "does not treat us as our sins deserve or repay us according to our iniquities." It is a comfort born of love, "as high as the heavens are above the earth." It removes our transgressions from us, "as far as the east is from the west." It is the profound comfort prophesied by Isaiah and long awaited by God's chosen people: "Comfort, comfort my people, says your God. Speak tenderly to Jerusalem" (Isaiah 40:1); "Proclaim the year of the LORD's favor and the day of vengeance of our God, to comfort all who mourn" (61:2). "The comfort promised in this beatitude is the ultimate consolation and encouragement that God alone can effect for those whose mourning expresses their sense of total loss and helplessness. It is a part of the future consummation when God will destroy sin and death and wipe away all tears."⁹

David honestly mourned what he had done, which is very different from feeling pity for what he had become. He tried to understand his actions but he did not excuse them. He was truly filled with remorse and repentance. Did Jesus have David in mind when he said, "Come to me all you who are weary and burdened and I will give you rest"? Yes, indeed. Was the second beatitude intended for David? Most certainly. Whether there is an empty six-pack in the trunk or some leftover crucifixion spikes in our pockets, we all need to repent and turn to Christ for forgiveness. For only then can we begin to experience the comfort we need.

It was not easy for David to mourn the way he did, but anything less would have been self-defeating. Excuses can be a terrible burden and self-justification only a quick fix. It was the forgiveness of Christ that turned David's mourning into rejoicing. It was the comfort promised by Jesus that made him a husband and father again. Through mourning, David learned the meaning of the easy yoke.

"*Y*ou're blessed when you feel you've lost what is most dear to you. Only then can you be embraced by the One most dear to you."

MATTHEW 5:4, *THE MESSAGE*

"*Blessed are the meek, for they will inherit the earth.*"

Matthew 5:5

CHAPTER FOUR

Willed Passivity

If you've ever wondered whether Jesus was the greatest idealist who ever lived, the third beatitude may have confirmed your suspicion. "Blessed are the meek, for they will inherit the earth." I'm surprised Peter didn't interrupt and say, "Excuse me, Master, did I hear You say, 'meek'? Didn't You mean, 'Blessed are the peak performers, for they will inherit the earth'?"

Is Jesus hopelessly naive? His advice seems out of place in the real-world rat race of power struggles, competition, and conflict. Don't the meek end up on the bottom of the heap? As one bumper sticker put it, "The meek shall inherit the earth after the takers are through using it up."

But according to Jesus, everything we've ever been told about getting ahead in the world is wrong. The world says, "Believe in yourself." Jesus says, "Believe in me." The world says, "Strive to be number one." Jesus says, "The last shall be first, and the first shall be last." The world says, "Winning isn't everything, it's the only thing." Jesus says, "He who finds his life will lose it, and he who loses his life for my sake will find it." The world says, "Don't get mad, get even." Jesus says, "Love your enemy and pray for those who persecute you." The world teaches, "Stand up for your rights." Jesus teaches, "Lay down your life." The world teaches us to assert ourselves; Jesus teaches us to deny ourselves. The world teaches us how to get ahead; Jesus teaches how to give ourselves away. The world says the one with the most toys wins; Jesus says, "You can gain the whole world and lose your soul."

We can't help but question if the strategy of Jesus helps us to live responsibly and realistically in American culture. Meekness sounds a lot like weakness. Pastor Don McCullough writes,

> Meekness. Let's admit it: we don't like the word. It tastes insipid, smells like morning-mouth, and looks like Caspar Milquetoast; it has the strength of a cooked noodle. Coaches don't rally teams with it; executives don't send sales people into the field with it; politicians don't promise to lead by it; parents don't counsel children to develop it; generals don't embolden troops with it. You won't find anyone offering seminars on meekness training. It probably should be examined by the House Committee on Un-American Activities. Or so we think.[1]

JESUS-STYLE MEEKNESS

To be poor in spirit is to know in our heart of hearts that we really need God. To mourn is to grieve deeply for our own guilt and to sorrow for our sinfulness. Wisely understood, the first two beatitudes are neither idealistic nor platitudinous. They are simple, profound truths that when acknowledged, personally and practically, help us live life the way it should be lived in dependence upon God. The strategy of Jesus for living in the real world begins with humility, not pride; repentance, not pity.

The third beatitude, meekness, has more to do with how we view the world and our role in it than it does with a personality type. It is a mind-set not a mood. To be meek is to believe the truth about how we are to relate to the world; it is not a temperament describing how we feel about it. In no way does meekness suggest weakness or softness. Meekness does not mean being laid-back, easygoing, tolerant, or laissez-faire. On the contrary, it requires conviction and strength. There is nothing superficial about the meekness blessed by Jesus. Our first impression of the third beatitude is wrong; the word *meekness* just doesn't translate well in our culture. Yet it is crucial to how we think about the Christian life.

The modern word for *meekness* in the American vocabulary is *passivity*. And most people think of passivity as a personality disorder. Passivity describes someone who feels inadequate, inferior, and helpless. Clinical psychologist Ronald Rottschafer writes,

> Passivity is born of anxiety; it is fear of using our energies lest we risk disapproval by others or risk failure in our own eyes. Passivity is a failure to mobilize our resources because we are afraid of consequences we do not think we could handle. It is a disowning of our nobler part—our self-reliance, our courage under fire, our resolve to win, our determination to inspire others to greater heights. Passivity is an abandonment of our inherent or acquired skills. . . . Passivity is an avoidance of our will, a problem called by Rollo May "an endemic of disease in the middle of the twentieth century . . . that saps us of our ability to make decisions, undermines our experience of ourselves as being responsible, and renders us as ethically impotent."[2]

Some Christians might assume erroneously that the third beatitude approves a docile, dependent personality. That somehow it is holier to feel inadequate and inferior. Wrongly understood, meekness makes a virtue of being the underdog, promoting a Rodney Dangerfield approach to living the Christian life. Many falsely assume that becoming the world's doormat is the cross Christians are called to bear. But this is not what Jesus intended by the character quality of meekness.

Meekness is an intentional reliance upon God to accomplish His will and His work in His way. "I tell you the truth," Jesus said, "the Son can do nothing by himself; he can do only what he sees his Father doing, because whatever the Father does the Son also does. . . . By myself I can do nothing" (John 5:19,30). Meekness is a "conscious suppression of willfulness and a purposeful cultivation of willingness."[3] It is an openness to see God in the big picture of life and the recognition "that in all things God works for the good of those who love him, who have been called according to his purpose" (Romans 8:28). Meekness leads us to say with Paul, "I can do all things through Christ who strengthens me," and mean it not as a boast but a confidence. Think of meekness as bold humility or aggressive patience. It is the spiritual discipline that overcomes the world.

SNAPSHOTS OF MEEKNESS
It is better to *see* meekness than simply hear about it. We need models, not theories. And the Bible is a rich depository of examples of meekness. We meet meekness in Abel and we meet its opposite in Cain. Sons of Adam and Eve, these two brothers chose different ways to approach God. To those unacquainted with the human need for repentance, forgiveness, and redemption, Cain's gift of the fruit of his labor may appear just as good, if not better, than Abel's sacrificial lamb. But the two offerings reveal the difference between pride and meekness; self-righteousness and repentance.

Self-directed Cain came to God on his own terms, using the occasion of worship as an opportunity for self-expression. Abel came to God humbly, letting his sacrificial lamb express his repentant heart. Cain stiffens against God's expectation; Abel bows before the Lord God, seeking deliverance, not compliments. Cain wants affirmation and recognition. The sin that should have led him to the altar with an offering of repentance rather than a token of his success masters Cain's heart, and he kills his brother.

We meet meekness in Abraham and its opposite in Lot. Abraham, the father of Israel and the recipient of God's blessing, felt no need to compete against his nephew, Lot. When conflict arose over grazing land for their herds, Abraham meekly concedes, "Let's not have any quarreling between you and me, for we are brothers. Is not the whole land before you? Let's part company. If you go to the left, I'll go to the right; if you go to the right, I'll go to the left." By all rights Abraham had the privilege of choice; all the land was his, but he gladly gave up that right for the sake of peace. There is no hint of possessiveness or arrogance in Abraham.

The two men stand before the land, wilderness on one side and the well-watered plain of Jordan on the other. It is a choice not only of land but of cultures; counter-culture meekness on one side, cultural conformity on the other. Lot pitched his tents near Sodom. Abraham built an altar to the Lord at Hebron. Lot's choice was based on pride and pleasure, Abraham's concession was based on humility and peace. Lot sought to please himself, but Abraham pleased God. Lot's decision resulted in his destruction and his family's. Abraham's decision revealed his heart and opened up the promises of God. We see the promise of Jesus in the life of Abraham. "Whoever finds his life will lose it, and whoever loses his life for my sake will find it" (Matthew 10:39).

We meet meekness in Moses and its opposite in Miriam and Aaron. Moses was a shy man and a reluctant leader of Israel. We are told that "Moses was a very humble man, more humble than anyone else on the face of the earth" (Numbers 12:3). When attacked, Moses did not defend his leadership or promote his position. Even those closest to him were frustrated by Moses' passivity when his authority was challenged and threatened (Numbers 11:28-29). Miriam and Aaron made the mistake of assuming that apparent passivity was an opportunity for their own advancement. They judged Moses according to their own standard of competence and qualifications, failing to recognize God's hand in selecting Israel's leader.

They sought to usurp the authority of God and the leadership of Moses. As a result, the Lord took it as a personal attack against Himself, not Moses. It was the Lord, not Moses, who filled that leadership position. Therefore, the Lord challenged their boldness: "Why then were you not afraid to speak against my servant Moses?" (Numbers 12:8).

We meet meekness in David and its opposite in King Saul. Anointed by Samuel to succeed Saul, David was reduced to a fugitive trying to escape the grasp of Saul's army. He fled for his life with his band of loyal men. On two separate occasions David had it within his power to take the life of Saul. Once in a cave, where David was so close to Saul that he cut off a corner of Saul's robe (an act for which he was almost immediately conscience-stricken), and once with Abishai when he crept into Saul's encampment. The troops, including the guards, were asleep along with Saul. Abishai could not believe the golden opportunity: "Today God has delivered your enemy into your hands. Now let me pin him to the ground with one thrust of the spear; I won't strike him twice" (1 Samuel 26:8). But David refused: "Don't destroy him! Who can lay a hand on the LORD's anointed and be guiltless?" David would not preempt the work of God. "The LORD himself will strike him." Meekness, judged from outside the will and work of God, appears to be weakness . . . a failure of nerve, but it is just the opposite.

David captured the essence of willed passivity in Psalm 37 with action verbs. "Do not fret because of evil men. . . . Trust in the LORD and do good. . . . Delight yourself in the LORD. . . . Commit your way to the LORD and trust in him. . . . Be still before the LORD and wait patiently for him. . . . Refrain from anger and turn from wrath. . . . But the meek will inherit the land and enjoy great peace." This is a meekness born of trust, not anxiety.

Meekness lightens the load and reduces the burden. Jesus-style meekness makes the yoke of Christ easy. The spiritual discipline of willed passivity saves us from the burden of worried productivity, yet many Christians have yet to experience freedom from the performance trap. Spirituality shaped by meekness rescues us from a spiritual full-court press designed to prove that we are worthy of people's affirmation. Meekness cuts through the sloth and the busywork of religious activities and teaches us to rely on Christ rather than our own efforts.

Luke gives us a snapshot of meekness at work when he tells the story of Martha and Mary. These two sisters, both of whom were sincere in their desire to be with Jesus, respond differently. Martha relates to Jesus as a busy hostess serving a special guest, but Mary relates to Jesus as a disciple dependent on her Lord. Mary "sat at the Lord's feet listening to what he said. But Martha was distracted by all the preparations that had to be made." Out of frustration Martha complained to Jesus, "Lord, don't you care that my sister has left me to do the work by myself? Tell her to help me!" "Martha, Martha," Jesus answered, "you are worried and upset about many things, but only one thing is needed. Mary has chosen what is better, and it will not be taken away from her" (Luke 10:38-42). Martha, the classic example of worried productivity. Mary, the picture of willed passivity. To people immersed in meetings, committees, and programs, meekness may look like laziness, but Jesus redefined sloth.

One of the most striking examples of willed passivity is offered by one of the most forceful personalities in the Bible. John the Baptist puts to rest any misguided notion that meekness is weakness. From adolescence to adulthood he patiently submitted to the will of God, and throughout his public ministry he powerfully presented the Word of God. Everything about him was framed in reference to Christ. "After me will come one more powerful than I, the thongs of whose sandals I am not worthy to stoop down and untie" (Mark 1:7). Before friends and enemies, soldiers and slaves, kings and paupers, John declared a compelling message of repentance and judgment. "I am the voice of one calling in the desert, 'Make straight the way for the Lord'" (John 1:23). From beginning to end, John the Baptist's one-liner was the bottom line: "I must decrease, but he must increase." If we shared John's willed passivity, we would experience his passion for Christ. Under the easy yoke of Jesus, there is no more effective way of getting ahead in this world than through meekness, even if it provokes the Herods of the world to take off your head.

AN ANTIDOTE FOR SELFISH ACTIVISM

Meekness saves us from wrong-headed activism. Hilary of Tours taught that every Christian had to be constantly vigilant against what he called—"a blasphemous anxiety to do God's work for him."[4] It is tempting to make the ministry a vehicle for self-expression and an excuse for self-indulgence.

There are numerous incidents in the Bible that illustrate this sinful tendency to turn the work of God into our own work. Moses was unable to enter the Promised Land because he struck the rock even though God had explicitly commanded that he speak to the rock (Numbers 20). King Saul was removed from office because he usurped the prophet's authority. Out of fear of losing control of his troops, he proceeded to offer sacrifices instead of waiting for Samuel (1 Samuel 13). Uzzah lost his life because of his "irreverent act." He took hold of the Ark of the Covenant when the oxen transporting it stumbled. This act alone provoked the Lord's anger against him and he was immediately struck dead (2 Samuel 6). David's insistence on counting the fighting men of Israel and Judah resulted in a plague that killed seventy thousand people (1 Chronicles 21).

These incidents remain obscure and inscrutable to us apart from God's expressed concern that we remain stewards of His work, rather than becoming our own masters. They are powerful reminders that there is a terrible price to pay for willfulness.

The Apostle Peter's spiritual journey is a classic study in meekness training. If there was ever a wrongheaded activist, it was Peter. He definitely does not fit the personality profile we associate with meekness. Three incidents stand out to prove this. When Jesus asked the disciples, "Who do you say that I am?" Peter confessed, "You are the Christ, the Son of the Living God." Jesus commended Peter's Spirit-led confession and went on to explain His path to the cross. But Peter was so cocksure he knew what Jesus should have been saying that he stood up to Him and rebuked Him. "Never, Lord!" Peter's willful desire to control Jesus and assert his own agenda was immediately rebuffed. Jesus quickly put Peter in his place. "Out of my sight, Satan! You are a stumbling block to me; you do not have in mind the things of God, but the things of men."

Like so many of us, Peter felt everybody was entitled to his opinion. Silence was a compelling invitation for Peter to express himself. Even the overwhelming event of the Transfiguration, when Peter, James, and John witnessed the sudden supernatural transformation of Jesus' appearance, so that "his face shone like the sun, and his clothes became as white as the light," did not quell Peter's precocious comments. He said what didn't need to be said: "Lord, it is good for us to be here." He said what should not have been said: "If you wish, I will put up three shelters—one for you, one for Moses and one for Elijah" (Matthew 17:1-4).

Perhaps the hardest thing for Peter to do was simply to listen to Jesus. Peter reminds me of those who are emotionally involved in church work but fail to understand the work of the Church. We are all ready to do something, when all God wants us to do is be faithful. The voice from Heaven declared, "This is my Son, whom I love; with him I am well pleased. Listen to him!" (verse 5).

The most glaring example of Peter's wrongheaded activism took place in the Garden of Gethsemane when temple guards came to arrest Jesus. Peter played the hero. He drew his sword and struck one of the servants of the high priest, cutting off his ear. Immediately before the incident, Peter was unable to stay awake to pray. Shortly after the arrest, Peter was afraid to admit to a servant girl that he knew Jesus. If Peter had practiced willed passivity, he would have patiently prayed and clearly confessed. Instead he willfully and foolishly took up the sword.

Peter eventually learned by the Spirit to practice meekness. We see it at Pentecost and hear it in his preaching. We recognize it in his logic before the religious leaders, "Judge for yourselves whether it is right in God's sight to obey you rather than God. For we cannot help speaking about what we have seen and heard" (Acts 4:19-20).

One of the clearest illustrations of Peter's willed passivity was his experience of the gospel's advance to the Gentiles. It would be hard for us to overestimate the gulf between Jew and Gentile in Peter's day. The same disciple who had not really heard Jesus on the subject of the Resurrection failed to grasp the universal, global significance of the good news of Jesus to all people.

When Peter received the vision revealing a smorgasbord of unclean animals a faithful Jew would not even think of eating, he surely thought he was having a nightmare. He responded to the voice in his dream commanding him to eat by shouting out, "Surely not, Lord!" Peter woke in theological shock, wondering what this dream, replayed two more times, had to do with him. He did not have long to wait for an answer. There was a knock on the door and the Spirit affirmed that the men standing there, sent from a Gentile named Cornelius, were sent by God. Peter invited them into his home as his guests. The next day he traveled with them to Caesarea to see Cornelius.

The whole episode is a study in willed passivity. This opinionated, self-willed, Galilean fisherman, who wanted to do things his way, had become willingly obedient and faithfully sensitive to the prompting of the Holy Spirit. Follow the dialogue in Acts and witness a transformation of attitude that is best described as meekness. Peter stands face to face with Cornelius, not knowing why he had traveled there, but knowing that God was in control. He knows that it is against Jewish law to associate with Gentiles, but God has just shown him that he should not call anyone impure or unclean. "May I ask why you sent for me?" Peter asks. Cornelius recounts his vision, expressing his willingness to hear the message that Peter has for him and his family. There is no resistance on Peter's part, not even surprise, only the humble acceptance that God is at work and "that God does not show favoritism, but accepts people from every nation who fear him and do what is right."

Even as Peter was preaching the gospel, the Holy Spirit came on all those who were hearing the message. To everyone's astonishment the experience of Pentecost was repeated in a Gentile living room. What could Peter do but accept the obvious? "Can anyone keep these people from being baptized with water? They have received the Holy Spirit just as we have" (Acts 10). From beginning to end we see the third beatitude beautifully expressed in Peter's openness to the will of God.

THE POLITICS OF MEEKNESS
In today's political climate, the followers of Christ may need a special reminder of biblical meekness. Many well-intentioned believers advocate an aggressive, belligerent stand against what they have rightly concluded is a very evil culture. Increasingly Christians appear obsessed with those who, by biblical standards, are wicked.

Over the past decade some Christians have gone from aggressive confidence to alarmism and paranoia. In the early 1980s there was talk of "rousing the slumbering giant, mobilizing the moral majority," and "having enough votes to run the country." But in the 1990s Christians talk of being victimized and "stepped on." They complain of "Christian-bashing." Christians have gone from boasting of their political clout to feeling like a beleaguered minority needing to fight for their rights. Fear has replaced confidence and panic has removed peace. Christian leaders impose guilt to manipulate believers into action by charging them with the sins of the culture. The politics of Jesus are giving way to the politics of resentment and revenge.

But the meekness of Jesus replaces the manipulative aggressiveness of the world. "The gospel of Jesus Christ is more political than anyone imagines, but in a way that no one guesses."[5] The meekness of the Cross did not mean disengagement and withdrawal from the world. Jesus did not escape the world; He refused to practice politics as usual. He ran from the crowd that wanted to make Him king, and He turned down Satan's offer of the kingdoms of the world. "My kingdom is not of this world," he declared to Pilate. "If it were, my servants would fight to prevent my arrest"(John 18:36).

The meekness of Jesus was not a mildness of disposition, but a total submission of direction. He taught us "to leave everything—ourselves, our rights, our causes, our whole future—in the hands of God."[6] We are reminded repeatedly by the apostles of how we are to approach the world.

> As a prisoner for the Lord, then, I urge you to live a life worthy of the calling you have received. Be completely humble and gentle; be patient, bearing with one another in love. (Ephesians 4:1-2)

> But in your hearts set apart Christ as Lord. Always be prepared to give an answer to everyone who asks you to give the reason for the hope that you have. But do this with gentleness and respect, keeping a clear conscience, so that those who speak maliciously against your good behavior in Christ may be ashamed of their slander. It is better, if it is God's will, to suffer for doing good than for doing evil. For Christ died for sins once for all, the righteous for the unrighteous, to bring you to God. (1 Peter 3:15-18)

Many of us would be freed of a tremendous load if we rediscovered the meaning of meekness. If we refused to fret because of evildoers and regained our confidence that God is in control. If we cultivated faith in the Lord Jesus rather than promoted fear. If we learned to forgive instead of retaliate.

Old Testament scholar Derek Kidner, commenting on Psalm 37 writes, "An obsession with enemies and rivals cannot be simply switched off, but it can be ousted by a new focus of attention; note the preoccupation with the Lord Himself, expressed in the four phases that contain His name here . . . a deliberate redirection of one's emotion (Paul and Silas in prison)."[7] Meekness is not dumb passivity nor timid advice. Biblical meekness is an aggressive force "in the battle raging between God and the devil. It requires high energy to meet the sword with willed suffering, with embraced sacrifice."[8]

Practicing the spiritual discipline of meekness changes not only how we operate politically, but also how we relate at home and at work. We discover how much more beneficial it is for us not to get uptight about our egos. Willed passivity drives out pettiness and small-minded obsessions with the larger view of Divine providence. We learn to avoid a false estimate of ourselves because we know we are sinners saved by God's grace.

By becoming meek, we refuse to manipulate and bully, not by being indifferent and apathetic, but by being honest and humble. We are free to cultivate a passion for God without panic. We can affirm God's truth passionately without an edge to our voice and a defensiveness in our tone. Like Mary, the first disciple, meekness opens us up to the will of God: "I am the Lord's servant. May it be to me as you have said" (Luke 1:38).

As I pointed out earlier, the Beatitudes are woven into the fabric of the Sermon on the Mount. Although we have only examined the first three beatitudes, I'll make references to all eight throughout this book. This powerful character description of a Christ-follower introduces us to and helps us comprehend everything else we'll discuss.

Remember that the Beatitudes are the primary colors mixed and blended with every shade of truth to follow. They color in the picture of what it means to take up the easy yoke. God's good Word spoken to us and over us, identifies us, shapes us, and rewards us. We understand who we are through the Word; the Beatitudes describe our character. In the confusion and chaos of what the world wants us to be, we receive gratefully the grace-filled Word of Jesus that is as comforting as it is convicting.

There is a definitive quality about the Beatitudes. They are not an opening monologue designed to pique people's interest or provoke discussion. They do not trigger debate or generate discussion. They are spoken with the finality of the last word. Yet this last word is also the first word. We end and begin with this benediction. We are not meant to become anything more or less than beatitude Christians.

The Greek word for benediction is *eulogia,* from which we get *eulogy,* literally meaning "good words." Traditionally, eulogies come at the end of one's life in memorial services, but these good words come at the beginning. Eulogies typically recount the best and most meaningful things in a person's life as we fondly remember achievements and relationships. But the Beatitudes celebrate the life we have received, not the life we have achieved. They remind us of God's providence, not of our performance.

As we move now to a discussion of the visible and hidden righteousness of the life of the disciple, we don't leave behind those blessings. Wherever we are in the Sermon, the commands and challenges, the choices and the convictions issue from our identity in Christ. We cannot practice love instead of hate, purity instead of lust, honesty instead of deception, without fitting the profile described in the Beatitudes. We cannot practice the hidden righteousness of giving, praying, and fasting without receiving the life given in the Beatitudes. We cannot make the single-minded choice for a true treasure, a true vision, and the true Master without the blessing of the Beatitudes. We cannot practice worry-free trust, nonjudgmental discernment, and faith-filled dependence without being blessed with the benediction of Jesus.

The Beatitudes set the tone that can be heard in the voice of Jesus throughout the Sermon, beginning with the believer's character and continuing with the believer's influence.

"*Y*ou're blessed when you're content with just who you are—no more, no less. That's the moment you find yourselves proud owners of everything that can't be bought."

MATTHEW 5:5, *THE MESSAGE*

"*You* are the salt of the earth. But if the salt loses its saltiness, how can it be made salty again? It is no longer good for anything, except to be thrown out and trampled by men.

"You are the light of the world. A city on a hill cannot be hidden. Neither do people light a lamp and put it under a bowl. Instead they put it on its stand, and it gives light to everyone in the house. In the same way, let your light shine before men, that they may see your good deeds and praise your Father in heaven."

MATTHEW 5:13-16

Salt and Light Disciples

Jesus did not doubt that the essential character of the disciple, described in the Beatitudes, resulted in a profound personal public impact. Having pronounced the blessing, He declares our responsibility; having established our identity, He describes our influence by using salt and light metaphors to describe the difference Christ makes in our lives. Jesus does not say, "You should be salt and you should be light." Nor does He say as the Reformers would have said, "You have the salt and you have the light" (meaning that they had the Word of God). Instead He declares, "You are the salt of the earth. . . . You are the light of the world."

One of the great "salt and light" Christians of the eighteenth century was John Wesley. He traveled over 250,000 miles on horseback through England, Scotland and Wales, preaching an estimated 40,000 sermons. Commenting on Matthew 5, Wesley wrote, "I shall endeavor to show, that Christianity is essentially a social religion; and that to turn it into a solitary religion, is indeed to destroy it." Not only is a private faith "absolutely contrary to the design of its great Author," but it is impossible according to Wesley. If true faith "abides in our hearts, it is impossible to conceal it."[1]

But true faith *does* abide in the heart and people *do*

71

manage to conceal it. Take the example of the man who trusted in Christ and determined to share his newfound faith with his friend at work. They had been colleagues for several years and their relationship was close. He prayed for the best time and the right words to tell his associate. Over lunch one day he decided to share what had happened to him. He carefully explained his commitment to Christ to his coworker. His coworker sat there nodding his head, listening intently to his story, then he interjected, "I'm so glad you have accepted Christ. I've been a Christian for years." The new Christian was surprised to say the least. How could his coworker have been a Christian for all these years without sharing his faith?

KEEP YOUR OPINION TO YOURSELF!

We face a great pressure in today's culture to make a person's commitment to Christ a private matter, an affair of the heart, something that is inwardly focused between the individual self and God. Since the center of authority in today's culture is the self, matters dealing with faith and belief are customized to fit everyone according to their likes and dislikes. Americans, even many professing believers, are not eager to submit to the authority of God's Word in their personal lives, let alone to encourage public recognition of God's truth in their social lives.

There are several reasons for this privatization of faith:

1. In a technologically oriented, market-centered, media-conditioned culture it is convenient to compartmentalize life. What a person believes about God has little relevance to university studies, finding a job, or enjoying life. Many people may think of themselves as Christians but this private religious sentiment has virtually nothing to do with choosing a spouse, clarifying their values, or prioritizing the use of their time. Most everything in life is shaped by secular culture.

2. Another factor is the presupposition that what a person believes about God falls into the subjective realm of knowledge. It is "soft" as opposed to "hard" objective knowledge, because it is based on feelings not facts. Secular culture, supposedly, bases knowledge on measurable, quantitative facts—economic figures, scientific facts, sociological polls. Everything else is private opinion.

3. Dogmatic relativism rules the day under the user-friendly labels of pluralism, diversity, and tolerance. The one thing that will not be tolerated is someone who believes God has spoken authoritatively. Every belief and ideology is acceptable, but one. The conviction that God's redemptive and moral truth is true for all people everywhere, whether a person acknowledges it or not, is judged exclusive, intolerant, and bigoted. Biblical revelation insists that "All truth is indeed God's truth," but secular culture holds that "Everybody's truth is truth."

4. Modern interpretations of the constitutional separation of church and state have led to the disestablishment of religion in public life. Even the simplest expressions of faith in Christ are judged inadmissible in the public sphere because they might violate the rights of others.

Followers of Jesus are pressured to be quiet about their faith and accept the prevailing cultural idea that religion is a private matter between you and God. The cultural message comes through loud and clear: Keep your opinion to yourself.

Tim Stafford, in an article in *Christianity Today* magazine, wrote:

Late in 1992, 14-year-old Christine Fisher was given a written assignment—"What Christmas Means to Me and Why"—for her computer class at Hill Country Middle School in Austin, Texas. Her teacher, Tom Roudebush, promised the class he would select the best essays for the school's newspaper. Christine was excited when she learned that her essay had been chosen. Principal Joe Bartlett, however, sent word that he could only publish the essay if Christine agreed to some changes. He wanted "It is also the day that Christians celebrate Christ's birth" altered to "It is also a day that people celebrate love." When Christine's father talked to Bartlett, [the principal] was unbending, citing "legal reasons." He said he was not censoring Christine, but using "editorial license."[2]

I remember my first experience of this not-so-subtle cultural message. My tenth grade, high school English class had a unit in public speaking. We were asked to give a fifteen-minute speech to our classmates on the subject of our choice. Most of these speeches were given to a class of about thirty students. Once a week, however, we met in a large lecture hall that seated several hundred students. Unfortunately, if your name fell on the day class was held in the large lecture hall, you spoke to the combined sections of all the English classes. Getting up in front of people is hard enough, but to do it before a couple hundred of your teenage peers was more of a challenge than I aspired for. The speech teacher told us that we could pick whatever subject we wanted to speak on. So after some careful thought I chose my subject: "The Most Important Thing in Life to Me" was my working title.

I remember struggling with this speech, hoping that I could communicate to my peers the importance of Jesus Christ. As you might have guessed, the day came for me to deliver my address and we were in the large lecture hall. After it was all over I felt as satisfied and relieved as I had felt nervous. Student feedback was very encouraging. All five students who were assigned to grade my speech gave it an A, but the speech teacher gave it a D. She was provoked that I had used that occasion to talk about Christ. I had violated her unwritten rule that religion is a private matter, best kept between yourself and God. Students had not found it offensive, even though most of them were not followers of Jesus. But she had found it deeply offensive.

My English teacher, a tall, thin German man in his fifties, handed back my speech and grade report. I looked at five A's and one bold red D, which would have given me a C for the speech, since the teacher's grade was worth 50 percent. Everything the students said as they rated style, content, and delivery was positive, while everything the speech teacher said was negative. My English teacher muttered under his breath to me, "I didn't count the D. The speech you gave was good."

SALT AND LIGHT IMPACT

From the days of the early Church, knowing Christ personally meant impact publicly. Jesus intended for Beatitude Christians to be the salt of the earth and the light of the world. Jesus directed the attention of his small group of disciples to the world. He guided them to pray, "Our Father in heaven, hallowed be your name, your kingdom come, your will be done on earth as it is in heaven" (Matthew 6:9-10).

He commissioned them to "Go and make disciples of all nations" (Matthew 28:19). He prayed to the Father, "As you sent me into the world, I have sent them into the world" (John 17:18). "The disciples . . . must not only think of heaven; they have an earthly task as well," writes Bonhoeffer. "Now that they are bound exclusively to Jesus they are told to look at the earth whose salt they are."[3]

One of the early church fathers, Justin Martyr, described the social changes brought about by the gospel: "Christian conversion meant the change from fornication to chastity, from magical arts to God, from acquisitiveness to sharing of goods, from hatred and exclusiveness to hospitality, prayer for enemies, and the wish to persuade those who are hostile to participate in Christian hope and joy."[4] According to Justin it was the patience and integrity of believers that drew people to consider the gospel of Christ. "Many have been led to 'change their violent and tyrannical disposition' and become Christians, 'being overcome either by the extraordinary forbearance they have observed in their fellow-travellers when defrauded, or by the honesty of those with whom they transacted business.'"[5]

Another early Christian, by the name of Diogenetus, gives us a moving description of the Christian life:

> Christians are distinguished from other people neither by country, nor language, nor customs which they observe. They follow the customs of the natives in respect to clothing, food, and the rest of their ordinary conduct, they display to us their wonderful and confessedly striking (paradoxical) method of life.
>
> They dwell in their own countries, but simply as sojourners. As citizens they share in all things with others, and yet endure all things as if foreigners. Every foreign land is to them as their native country, and every land of their birth as a land of strangers. They marry, as do all; they beget children; but they do not destroy their offspring. They have a common table, but not a common bed. They are in the flesh, but they do not live after the flesh. They pass their days on earth, but they are citizens of heaven. They obeyed the prescribed laws, and at the same time surpass the laws by their lives.
>
> They love all men, and are persecuted by all. They are unknown, yet condemned. . . . They are poor, yet make many rich. . . . They are dishonored, and yet in their dishonor are glorified. They are evil spoken of, and yet are justified; when reviled they bless. To sum up all in one word—what the soul is in the body, that is what Christians are in the world.

The soul is dispersed through all the members of the
body, and Christians are scattered through all the cities
of the world. The soul dwells in the body, yet is not of
the body . . . ; the soul loves the flesh that hates it,
Christians likewise love those that hate them. The soul
is imprisoned in the body, yet preserves ("keeps
together") that very body, and Christians are confined in
the world as in a prison, and yet they are the preservers
of the world.[6]

Ancient Christians expected they would be counter-
cultural. To be a follower of Jesus meant living a quality of life
that was impossible to conceal, simply because it affected
everything in life, from family to work and from sexuality to
spirituality. The meaning of Jesus' salt and light metaphors was
played out in daily life.

The inherent qualities of salt and light give shape and direction to the public impact of the follower of Jesus. As salt prevents decay, light dispels darkness. "Jesus calls his disciples to
exert a double influence on the secular community, a negative
influence by arresting its decay and a positive influence by
bringing light into its darkness."[7] Preservation and illumination
describe the influence of the Christian. This implies of course,
the obvious truth, that the world needs help. Decay and darkness are realities, not surprises!

Jesus intended for His followers to penetrate their culture
the way salt was rubbed into meat to prevent it from going bad.
Jesus does not say, "You are the sugar of the earth" or "You are
the honey of the world." German theologian, Helmut
Thielicke, speaks of the biting quality of true Christian witness:
There is a natural temptation for Christians "to sweeten and
sugar the bitterness of life with an all too easy conception of a
loving God."[8] Are we too sweet for the world's own good? Have
we become so accepting and accommodating that there is no
resistance to the world going bad?

Since refrigeration has replaced salt as our culture's chief means of preserving food, we now think of salt as a flavor enhancer; it is a condiment, not an essential commodity. In fact it's a suspect condiment, because too much salt may be bad for your heart. There is an apparent metamorphosis in meaning for the Christian as well. By adding just a little flavor to a pluralistic society, today's Christian acts as a flavor enhancer. But Jesus expected His disciples to be an essential preservative, vital to the world's survival. And in some circles the Christian's influence is about as popular as salt in a salt-free diet. The believer's salty influence may not be appreciated by the world, but what is absolutely crucial is that followers of Jesus see their role as a necessary preservative. Being the salt of the earth is not an option a Christ-follower can decline.

The metaphor of light has also undergone a change. It is difficult for us to imagine living without the convenience of electrical light. When Jesus spoke the words "You are the light of the world," there was only one light to speak of, the light of the sun. Today we popularly think of turning on "artificial" light. We forget how really dependent we still are on sunlight.

Everyone in the audience knew what Jesus meant when He spoke of light. Light meant revelation; the darkness was illuminated by the truth of God.

> Your word is a lamp to my feet
>> and a light for my path. (Psalm 119:105)

> The unfolding of your words gives light;
>> it gives understanding to the simple.
>>> (Psalm 119:130)

> The precepts of the LORD are right,
>> giving joy to the heart.
> The commands of the LORD are radiant,
>> giving light to the eyes. (Psalm 19:8)

Send forth your light and your truth,
   let them guide me;
let them bring me to your holy mountain,
   to the place where you dwell. (Psalm 43:3)

For these commands are a lamp, this teaching is a light,
   and the corrections of discipline are the way to life.
      (Proverbs 6:23)

First-century Gnostics used the metaphor of light to speak of secret, mystical, intuitive sources of truth. They come the closest to the modern idea, which is so popular today, that everyone lives according to his own light. Who needs the light of the sun when you can flip the switch of your own light? Today's adage is: What's true for you may not be true for me. Even among professing Christians, the light of God's revelation often stands as a lesser light to the light of conventional morality, popular science, or pop-psychology.

However, being popular is not what Jesus had in mind. Jesus said, "I am the light of the world. Whoever follows me will never walk in darkness, but will have the light of life" (John 8:12). His followers reflect that light, even though others resist it. Saint John gave this verdict: "Light has come into the world, but men loved darkness instead of light because their deeds were evil. Everyone who does evil hates the light, and will not come into the light for fear that his deeds will be exposed" (John 3:19-20).

Disciples are meant to take seriously the pronouncement of Jesus: They are not flavor enhancers, spicing up the diversity of the world, nor are they optional lighting for those who prefer a different shade of meaning. They are the salt of the earth and the light of the world. Not because they are something special in themselves, but because Jesus said they are.

Appearances can be deceiving. The followers of Jesus have all sorts of jobs but only one vocation. When asked what she did for a living, one bright believer described herself as a disciple of Jesus Christ carefully disguised as computer pro-grammer. Secular saints may work in construction or banking or medicine or education or baking, but they serve as Christ's ambassadors. We are all tent-makers of one kind or another, serving as little apostles. Fulfilling this vocation, as Eugene Peterson points out, can be dangerous work.

> What is hazardous in my life is my work as a Christian. Every day I put faith on the line. I have never seen God. In a world where nearly everything can be weighed, explained, quantified, subjected to psychological analy-sis and scientific control, I persist in making the center of my life a God whom no eye hath seen, nor ear heard, whose will no one can probe. That's a risk.[9]

RADICAL SUBVERSIVES FOR THE KINGDOM OF GOD
Daniel provides an excellent case study in the challenges of vocational holiness. In the fifth century before Christ, Neb-uchadnezzar conquered Jerusalem. As part of his program of assimilation, he selected well-qualified young men from the Jewish upper class for special training. Daniel became an ancient equivalent to today's Rhodes Scholar. His intensive educational indoctrination involved total immersion in Baby-lonian culture. He was placed under the charge of a foreign official, given a foreign name, called by a foreign title, instructed in a foreign language, and offered a foreign diet.

Daniel's situation was not unlike our own. We find our-selves immersed in a culture where we don't feel at home. The values, priorities, commitments, and beliefs are foreign to the gospel of Jesus Christ. We are aliens and sojourners "look-ing forward to the city with foundations, whose architect and builder is God" (Hebrews 11:10).

Daniel excelled in his new habitat, but he resolved not to defile himself. He took a stand against assimilating into Baby-lonian culture by abstaining from the court diet. It was a strategic act of obedience to God designed to preserve his identity as a Hebrew in Nebuchadnezzar's court.

By outward appearances Daniel was a professional in a corporate culture, but in reality he was a radical subversive for the Kingdom of God. His wisdom and integrity provoked the envy and anger of his colleagues. We remember Daniel as a man of prayer, whose consistency in communion with God three times a day became the only thing his enemies could think of to use against him. They were unable to find any corruption in the way he handled his government affairs. Their complaint was his commendation: "We will never find any basis for charges against this man Daniel unless it has something to do with the law of his God" (Daniel 6:5).

Daniel's integrity was more than a simple matter of professional honesty. His budgets were accurate, his disclosures were reliable, his memos dependable. But beyond this professional standard was the radical honesty of the prophet who declared the Word of God boldly even when it might have jeopardized his career. Daniel's inner self was driven by a vision of the future of God's salvation. He knew that the life he lived in the Babylonian court was not his destiny. He never confused Babylon with heaven (7:13-14). He may have looked the part of the successful professional, but friends and enemies alike knew him to be what he really was: a man of God, salt and light in a pagan culture. His career in the Babylonian court spanned seventy years, but we remember him the way the New Testament describes him, as a prophet of the Word of God (Matthew 24:15).

A contemporary example of someone with "salt and light" impact is Charles Glenn, the director of Equal Educational Opportunities for the Massachusetts Department of Education. He advises Christians how to be salt and light in the public school system.

- ◆ Recognize that we live in a very diverse, pluralistic culture. Approach correction and change from the principle of fairness rather than favoritism.

- Review curriculum and propose modification or enrichment to ensure fairness.

- Propose optional mini-courses around issues of interest to some students and staff.

- Provide educational enrichment programs occurring outside of school during school hours.

- Take an extra half-hour of homework time to review assigned readings and discuss them in the light of faith.

- Be thankful for the challenge. "If we may deplore the fact that our postmodern society is incoherent with respect to values, we may also celebrate the fact that many of our contemporaries are searching for values and belief for themselves and their children. There can be no better place to meet a secularized society with tolerance and respect, but also with clarity about our essential convictions, than in public schools."[10]

Another example is physician Thomas Elkins, an obstetrician/gynecologist and professor at the University of Tennessee Medical Center. The father of a young child with Down's syndrome, Dr. Elkins has devoted himself to developing a case for Christian ethics in situations where parents of newborns are faced with the reality of a handicapped infant. He is involved in the American Academy of Pediatrics task force on the formation of hospital ethics committees and is active on the national ethics committee of the American College of Obstetricians and Gynecologists. He is on the front line struggling with difficult ethical questions.

Elkins says, "The Sermon on the Mount is a very motivational approach to ethics. Ethics is not constant rule making but an understanding of what Christ would have you do in an individual situation. We must learn to bring Christian values into the systems that are with us here and now. We can't go back to the year 1200. The Lord has allowed us to develop the technologies of today, and it is our responsibility to use them in a framework of Christian principles."[11]

Asked if he was optimistic about the future, Elkins responded, "Yes. Maybe that sounds crazy, but I am. It's like reading the Book of Habakkuk. If the last four verses in that book were missing, what a tragedy life would be. We've all stood there and screamed at the sky and said, 'When's this going to stop? When is something going to work here?' There are answers; there is hope, and hope lies within our ability as Christian people to keep in touch with God through a personal relationship with him. He allows us to be optimistic. He allows us to hope."[12]

Some Christians at Harvard are also taking their salt and light responsibility seriously. They conduct a seminar entitled the "Harvard Evangelical Laity Involvement Exercises" or "Helix" for short. They have developed ten workshop sessions on such issues as a theology of vocation, lordship, evangelism, contemplative disciplines, basic theology, social justice, church responsibilities, and family and interpersonal relationships.

At the end of the seminar, participants write a paper answering the following questions:

1. How has your choice of a career in a particular vocation been governed by the values of the Kingdom and your unique gifts and abilities?

2. What are your overall objectives as a missionary to your chosen vocational discipline?

3. What are the specific areas in which your vocational discipline is hostile to the gospel? Friendly to the gospel?

4. What kind of evangelistic ministry do you intend to have with those who work in proximity to you?

5. What kind of discipling ministry do you hope to have with those Christians who share your vocational environment?

6. How will you balance the pressures on your time, particularly with regard to family and other relational responsibilities?[13]

PART-TIME DISCIPLES

The Harvard "salt and light" seminar assumes that it is more fulfilling and meaningful to live yoked to Jesus in every aspect of life than it is to live a compartmentalized, privatized faith. The yoke is easy and the burden light *if* our faith in Christ is central to everything we do. But Jesus warns His disciples that salt and light can be wasted. The salt can become contaminated and the light can be hidden.

Technically speaking, salt or sodium chloride does not break down easily. It is a very stable chemical compound. Since there were no refineries in Jesus' day, the "salt" He refers to was a mixture of sodium chloride and other chemicals. Because sodium chloride, the most soluble component, easily washed out in the rain, it was common for "salt" to become nothing more than road dust.[14] The people understood the common practice of keeping the salt dry and protecting it from contamination. It doesn't make sense to expose the salt to contamination, and it is foolish to conceal the light. Let the salt prevent decay and light dispel the darkness.

Last summer I was at a conference with the Canadian Christian Medical and Dental society. This group of seventy-five doctors and spouses devoted three hours in the morning to worship and Bible study. They impressed me as being much more patient and attentive to the Word of God than a group of pastors would have been. They truly enjoyed the worship. It was not something they were trying to get through and move on to the next thing. They were there to enjoy God.

Strangely enough, pastors have trouble praying leisurely. We become hyperactive, religiously speaking. We face the temptation of talking so much about God that we are no longer aware of God. It is always a great privilege to be among those who know that they are "salt and light" followers of the Lord Jesus. Their work in the secular world is holy, Kingdom work preserving the world from decay and dispelling the darkness. This is what a pastor friend of mine meant when he quipped, "After I pronounce the benediction, I don't want to see them for a week." He had no intention of filling their time with church programs and religious busywork when they needed to be about their Father's business of being salt and light.

We can lose our saltiness by following Jesus in our spare time, by turning full-time vocational holiness into a part-time extracurricular activity. When I was in college I took a part-time job as a night security guard at a new condominium complex that was under construction. I went to classes and studied all day, and I worked three nights a week from 7:00 p.m. to 5:00 a.m. The pay was good, but I learned after a few weeks that I just couldn't do it. I felt like a part-time student and full-time night watchman. I fell asleep in class and fell behind in my studies. In addition to losing sleep, I lost my concentration and my appetite. I realized that I would have to get another job, one that fit better with being a student. If the life of discipleship is too hard, it may be because we are adding things to our lives that do not fit well with following Jesus. Maybe we are trying to be part-time disciples.

Being a disciple of Jesus is not a hobby. We are not disciples the way we are members of the Sierra Club or Rotary. One does not take up the easy yoke the way one takes up golf. The Christian life becomes an impossible burden when it is lived part-time or approached halfheartedly. Following Jesus requires everything else in life to be integrated with our commitment to Christ.

A SALTY NATURE

There is a quality of living that flows naturally from being a disciple of Christ, and herein lies the secret of the easy yoke. Salt is salty by nature; its activity is inherent in its essence. Light automatically shines; illumination cannot be separated from what it is by definition. What salt and light do are perfectly consistent with what they are. This is true of many things in life, such as athletic ability in the athlete, musical expression in the musician, and parental love in the parent. No athlete would ever say being an athlete is easy; too much training, discipline, and determination are required to call it easy. But deny the slopes to the skier or the ice to the skater or the water to the swimmer and the deprivation is far more painful than the exertion. The musician finds it far more difficult to be deprived of her instrument than to put in additional hours of practice time. It's easier to fulfill her identity than to deny it or suppress it.

I am not suggesting that being an athlete or a musician is an identity comparable to being a follower of Christ. As we have seen in the Beatitudes, discipleship goes to the very essence of who we are and who we were made to be, in a way that sports or the arts are unable to satisfy. Nevertheless, these comparisons help us understand the nature of the easy yoke. There is an inherent quality of being in Christ that makes life easier to fulfill than to deny. Take away running from the runner, writing from the author, painting from the artist and you have not made their lives easier; you've made them harder.

This is true for the followers of Christ as well. A young mother cannot deny her child love; to do so would be unnatural and a violation of her spirit. Neither can a disciple of Jesus deny the righteousness of Christ without great pain and difficulty.

Who we are as salt and light comes from the grace of God working within, enabling us to practice the righteousness of Jesus. We are transformed and shaped by the blessing of God. By virtue of being yoked to Jesus we are empowered to live righteously. The hunger and thirst for righteousness comes from within. That is why Jesus says, "Let your light shine before people, that they may see your good deeds and praise your Father in heaven."

Everything Jesus asks His disciples to do in the Sermon on the Mount is natural to them. For disciples to do otherwise is to deny their true identity. It would be like asking the sailor to dislike the sea or the farmer to despise the land. For disciples to lose their saltiness or to conceal their light is to make life harder, not easier.

Having discussed the believer's identity (the Beatitudes) and influence (Salt and Light), in the next chapter we'll look at what Jesus says about the believer's "good deeds." In the Sermon on the Mount Jesus shows us the source and scope of true righteousness. Righteousness is not some vague, ethereal ethic, the nature of which may be defined by personal preference and taste. Jesus defines righteousness in a specific, definite way. We are not left to our imagination or invention, but to His revelation.

"*L*et me tell you why you are here. You're here to be salt-seasoning that brings out the God-flavors of this earth. If you lose your saltiness, how will people taste godliness? You've lost your usefulness and will end up in the garbage.

"Here's another way to put it: You're here to be light, bringing out the God-colors in the world. God is not a secret to be kept. We're going public with this, as public as a city on a hill. If I make you light-bearers, you don't think I'm going to hide you under a bucket, do you? I'm putting you on a light stand. Now that I've put you there on a hilltop, on a light stand—shine! Keep open house; be generous with your lives. By opening up to others you'll prompt people to open up with God, this generous Father in heaven."

MATTHEW 5:13-16, *THE MESSAGE*

"*Do* not think that I have come to abolish the Law or the Prophets; I have not come to abolish them but to fulfill them. I tell you the truth, until heaven and earth disappear, not the smallest letter, not the least stroke of a pen, will by any means disappear from the Law until everything is accomplished. Anyone who breaks one of the least of these commandments and teaches others to do the same will be called least in the kingdom of heaven, but whoever practices and teaches these commands will be called great in the kingdom of heaven. For I tell you that unless your righteousness surpasses that of the Pharisees and the teachers of the law, you will certainly not enter the kingdom of heaven."

MATTHEW 5:17-20

CHAPTER SIX

Setting the Record Straight

We live in a day and age when truth, along with relationships, has become a perishable commodity. Truth has the shelf-life of a dairy product. Our expectation of obsolescence in everything from celebrities to politicians, from cars to tennis shoes, from computers to communications, seems to be affecting our conviction about truth. When everybody's truth is truth, we change truth the way we change fashion. We rely more on public opinion polls than the authoritative Ten Commandments. Today's version of truth and righteousness reminds one more of a weather vane than a compass.

Current concepts of righteousness are much like contemporary definitions of art. If anything, modern art seems to defy definition. Art is anything you want it to be. It is art by virtue of the fact that it hangs in an art gallery or is done by an "artist."

Modern morality suffers the same fate. Contemporary ethics is shaped more by the ethos of a culture than the moral order revealed in God's Word. This is true in many churches as well. The Body of Christ is limp, without form or strength. The skeletal system is unable to support the weight of the body. A strong, healthy understanding of God's law has been replaced by a spineless compromise with the prevailing norms of culture.

The follower of Jesus needs to acknowledge the inseparable relationship between the Law and the gospel. The gospel must be preached so that the Law does not lead to despair. The Law must be preached so that the gospel does not lead to complacency.

We are tempted, particularly in American Christianity, to make the Law the enemy of the gospel. To some, grace gives the believer carte blanche to live as he or she pleases with the assurance that all is forgiven in Christ. Any mention of the Law is branded as legalism. One seldom hears among today's believers an earnest desire for purity and holiness. The virtues of peace and harmony are loudly promoted, but the quest for godliness sounds archaic and quaint. Sadly, the desire to be holy is sometimes frowned upon because it is considered synonymous with a "holier than thou" attitude.

When this is our attitude toward the Old Testament commandments, the Christian life becomes a frustrating burden. Bonhoeffer wrote, "The Christian life comes to mean nothing more than living in the world and as the world, in being no different from the world, in fact, in being prohibited from being different from the world for the sake of grace. The upshot of it all is that my only duty as a Christian is to leave the world for an hour or so on a Sunday morning and go to church to be assured that my sins are all forgiven. I need no longer try to follow Christ."[1]

There is a great deal of confusion over the believer's relationship to the law of God. Over the course of a year I met several times for lunch with a self-professed agnostic who was seriously considering the claims of Christ. His Christian friends at work passed along books by C. S. Lewis, Chuck Colson, and Philip Yancey for him to read. He interacted with these books and had dialogue with his Christian friends. He was definitely searching. He followed the Sunday morning message as closely as anyone in the congregation. When we met, our conversations centered not so much on the intellectual issues of faith and reason as much as on ethical concerns of faith and practice.

He claimed that the biggest hurdle he had to overcome was his wife, who was a believer. She had faithfully attended church for years and felt the problems in their marriage were rooted in the fact that he was not a Christian. One of the first questions he asked me was, "Do you believe it is right for my teenage daughter to invite her boyfriend home to spend the night in the same bed?" Before I could answer, he said, "My wife does. She believes that Jesus desires intimacy in relationships, so that it is okay for my daughter to sleep with her boyfriend. I'm sorry, but I think that's wrong. What do you think?"

This woman had used the love of Jesus to condone whatever behavior pattern their children had wanted to practice. Of course it is possible he was using his wife's perspective as an excuse for not becoming a believer. However, her feeling toward the moral law is not unusual in the American Church. By claiming that the unconditional love of Jesus approves immorality in the name of intimacy, she divorced law and gospel, forgiveness and obedience. For others, the excuse is diversity or tolerance, justifying sin in the name of Jesus.

NEITHER LIBERTINE NOR LEGALIST

For the sake of His disciples, not His critics, Jesus defines His relationship to the Law and the Prophets. "Do not think that I have come to abolish the Law or the Prophets; I have not come to abolish them but to fulfill them" (Matthew 5:17). From the tone and force of Jesus' statement, it is apparent that His detractors were spreading malicious rumors about Him. They claimed He did not respect the law of God; that He had in fact violated the Law by desecrating the Sabbath.

The religious leaders found Jesus' fresh, new perspective of the Law and Prophets threatening. It was easier for them to use the Law against Jesus than to understand how Jesus fulfilled the Law and the Prophets. No one would have dared to place himself in relationship to the Law the way Jesus did. For a scribe to hear Jesus say, "I have not come to abolish the Law and the Prophets but to fulfill them," sounded like unmitigated arrogance.

Perhaps the least controversial fact about Jesus is that He was a teacher, until you listen to His teaching! For unlike the rabbis, Jesus taught with absolute authority. Jesus initiated an entirely original stance toward the Law that implied a highly disputed, if not blasphemous, conclusion. The more He taught, the more obvious it became to the Jewish religious experts that Jesus saw Himself fulfilling and transcending the Old Testament law. No one, then or now, can read the Sermon on the Mount seriously and conclude that Jesus was simply a great moral teacher. He assumed an authority in relationship to the Law that was unique and unprecedented. Jesus' signature statement, "Truly, I say to you," or "I tell you the truth," was used by no other teacher. "It serves, like the prophets' 'Thus says the Lord,' to mark a saying as important and authoritative."[2]

Jesus pledged undivided loyalty to the Law, but in doing so He made Himself central to the Law's relevance. The authoritative "I" became the focus of attention. He did not come to destroy the Law but to fulfill it. By expounding the true meaning of the commandments, He offered the true measure of righteousness. Jesus' perspective on the Law is vitally important for Christians today. Without it, we are tempted to equate heartfelt obedience with letter-of-the-law legalism, or we end up reducing righteousness to a list of do's and don'ts. Neither the libertine nor the legalist is satisfied with Jesus.

ABSOLUTE OR OBSOLETE?
Unknowingly, many contemporary Christians favor the views of Marcion, a second-century theologian who tried to divorce the Old Testament from the New Testament. He believed that the God of the Old Testament was vindictive and judgmental. He claimed that the God of the Jews performed evil acts and was self-contradictory. According to Marcion, Jesus was not the fulfillment of Old Testament messianic prophecies, but a revelation of the God of love.[3] Marcion's ancient heretical thesis is

still popular today as self-designated "enlightened" Christians distance themselves from the commands and precepts of God's Word.

It is almost as if many modern Christians wished that the malicious rumors spread by the Pharisees were true of Jesus. It would be a relief for them to find that Jesus rendered the Old Testament commands obsolete. They would find it easier to believe that Jesus liberated people from the prescientific, anachronistic commands of the Bible than to think that Jesus lined up with the Law and Prophets. They confuse Jesus' resistance to the scribes and religious leaders with opposition to the moral order described in the statutes and precepts of the Old Testament. If Jesus were alive today, they contend, He would readily accept homosexual partnerships, deny the need for the sacrificial atonement of the Cross, approve premarital sex within intimate loving relationships, and trace society's problems to the domination of the white, middle class male.

It is precisely the false representation of Jesus' relationship to the Law and the Prophets that provoked His definitive reaction. Far from becoming obsolete, Jesus affirmed the Law to be absolute. "I tell you the truth, until heaven and earth disappear, not the smallest letter, not the least stroke of a pen, will by any means disappear from the Law until everything is accomplished" (Matthew 5:18). He could not have made His point more emphatically.

"The iota (the letter *yod*) is the smallest Hebrew letter, and is often optional in spelling; the dot (*keraia,* 'horn') may be either the similar letter *waw* (which is equally optional), or the *serif* which distinguishes some similar Hebrew letters. The rabbis discussed at length the destructive effects of such minute alterations to a single letter of the law."[4] In effect, Jesus was saying, "Trivialize even the smallest item in God's Law and you will only have trivialized yourself. But take it seriously, show the way for others, and you will find honor in the kingdom."[5] Absolutely nothing will be left out, dismissed, or rendered obsolete "until everything is accomplished."

THE HEART OF THE MATTER

Jesus came not to abolish the Law but to draw out the significance of the Law and to fulfill all that God intended through the Law. Jesus came to establish the Law, not undermine it; to complete it, not condemn it. By reducing it to an external religious authority and legal code, the Pharisees short-circuited the intended meaning of the Law. They were guilty of missing the meaning of the Law by substituting external religious conformity for heart righteousness.

Jesus was determined to set the record straight. His promise to fulfill the Law and Prophets is inclusive of everything the Old Testament taught, symbolized, modeled, and looked forward to. Jesus fulfilled the covenant promises made to Abraham and David. He accomplished everything anticipated in the burnt sacrifices, Passover lamb, and tabernacle. He exemplified the perseverance of Job and the faithfulness of Abraham. He embodied the goal of the Law espoused by the Prophets in His own righteousness. In every way—doctrinally, ethically, and ceremonially—the Law finds its completion in Jesus. All of this lies behind His concise affirmation, "Do not think that I have come to abolish the Law or the Prophets; I have not come to abolish them but to fulfill them."

Jesus did not approach the Law as an innovator but as its Author. He does not renegotiate the Law to His liking but interprets the Law according to its intended original meaning. The analogy used by C. S. Lewis helps to explain the central significance of Jesus to the Law.

> Let us suppose we possess parts of a novel or a symphony. Someone now brings us a newly discovered piece of manuscript and says, "This is the missing part of the work. This is the chapter on which the whole plot of the novel really turned. This is the main theme of the symphony." Our business would be to see whether the new passage, if admitted to the central place which the discoverer claimed for it, did actually illuminate all the

parts we had already seen and "pull them together." Nor should we be likely to go very far wrong. The new passage, if spurious, however attractive it looked at the first glance, would become harder and harder to reconcile with the rest of the work the longer we considered the matter. But if it were genuine, then at every fresh hearing of the music or every fresh reading of the book, we should find it settling down, making itself more at home, and eliciting significance from all sorts of details in the whole work which we had hitherto neglected. Even though the new central chapter or main theme contained great difficulties in itself, we should still think it genuine provided that it continually removed difficulties elsewhere. Something like this we must do with the doctrine of the Incarnation. Here, instead of a symphony or a novel, we have the whole mass of our knowledge. . . . We believe that the sun is in the sky at midday in summer not because we can clearly see the sun (in fact, we cannot) but because we can see everything else.[6]

In Jesus we find the key to interpreting the Law and the Prophets. Without Him we cannot get a true perspective on righteousness. He alone restored to biblical interpretation its original and intended purpose and set the Law in an entirely new theological context. He both established and transcended the meaning that had been lost by both the popular and the more rigorous biblical interpreters of His day.

The Pharisees understood Old Testament law the way a lawyer views a legal contract. A precise, nuance interpretation of the Law took on crucial significance. By scrutinizing the wording of the text and carefully considering the history of interpretation, the Pharisees were prepared to define the requirements of the Law in every conceivable situation. Scripture was the basis for a legal code, which required supplementing the biblical text with specific "bylaws" for conduct.

The problem, however, is that biblical obedience is not imposed by a contractual obligation, but inspired by a covenant relationship.

A prenuptial agreement tries to set out the obligations and understanding of a relationship in legal terms. Legal contingency plans are drawn up in case the relationship breaks up. How different such an arrangement is from a vowed commitment. Marriage depends upon a couple's covenant commitment to one another. They pledge themselves to one another unconditionally and unreservedly. The language of their vows is inclusive of all they are and will be. "As long as our lives shall last" is the bottom line of a costly vow.[7]

When Ginny and I decided it was time to draw up a will, we went to a lawyer. We wanted a simple will declaring that when one of us dies the other receives everything. And when we both die our property is to be divided equally among our three children. Nothing complicated, right? No. The lawyer drew up twelve pages of single-spaced legal wording in fine print covering every kind of contingency. The legal language was so technical I had to keep asking him for a translation. That legal document is now filed away along with old tax returns and appliance warranties. It has absolutely no effect on my daily life. It is there if a lawyer needs to prove what should take place normally at our deaths.

It was a different story when Ginny and I were married. We did not sign a contract, we made a commitment. Before God and in the presence of family and friends we exchanged vows. We did not debate the intricacies of a legal contract covering all the possible contingencies that could affect our marriage, though ultimately such contingencies are far more complex and challenging than any that might affect disposal of wealth. We committed ourselves to each other in unguarded, unqualified, comprehensive language. The vows I made on that day affect every day of my life. Those few simple words expressed once and for all the desire of my heart to be committed to one and only one woman forever. I can renew my vows, but I cannot add to their lasting effect.

Of all the things Jesus said about the Law, the most startling assertion must have been His ultimatum: "For I tell you that unless your righteousness surpasses that of the Pharisees and the teachers of the law, you will certainly not enter the kingdom of heaven." The first thought of the disciples may have been, "How could anyone be more scrupulous in observing the Law than the Pharisees?" Meeting the prescribed standard of the Law, right down to tithing one's herbs and spices, must have seemed an impossible burden to a Galilean fisherman, a former tax collector, and a political zealot. Jesus took them by surprise. The disciples knew that when it came to compliance with the Law, they were not in the same league with the Pharisees.

The second thought of the disciples must have been that Jesus meant to revolutionize their understanding of the Law. With all the authority of the Law's creator, Jesus calls for a righteousness that "far surpasses pharisaic righteousness in kind rather than in degree."[8] Obedience was not an exacting compliance to a list of rules, but a heartfelt commitment to the will of God. True obedience could not be measured in a court of law but in the mind of God.

Does this mean that the commands and statutes of the Law could be quietly laid aside in favor of an interior, private religion ruled by the dictates of one's own heart? No way! It is only in Jesus that we begin to realize the full extent of the psalmist's words: "The law of the LORD is perfect, reviving the soul. The statutes of the LORD are trustworthy, making wise the simple. The precepts of the LORD are right, giving joy to the heart. The commands of the LORD are radiant, giving light to the eyes" (Psalm 19:7-8). Jesus is more liberating than liberals, who misconstrue freedom as promiscuity and license, and more radical than the conservatives, who misunderstand obedience as conformity to a selective list of do's and don'ts. Jesus roots righteousness in God's passion for us and in our passion for God.

Jesus wrote the final chapter on the Law. In Christ, the promise of God is fulfilled, which was given through the prophet Jeremiah:

> "This is the covenant I will make with the house of Israel after that time," declares the LORD. "I will put my law in their minds and write it on their hearts. I will be their God, and they will be my people. No longer will a man teach his neighbor, or a man his brother, saying, 'Know the LORD,' because they will all know me, from the least of them to the greatest," declares the LORD. "For I will forgive their wickedness and will remember their sins no more." (Jeremiah 31:33-34)

The story is told of a young boy who was fascinated by the work of a sculptor. The artist had begun a new project on a huge block of marble. He chiseled and filed, working the stone into the desired shape. Daily the young boy came to watch. Slowly and painstakingly the marble was being transformed before his very eyes. After several weeks had gone by and the work of the sculptor was almost complete, the young boy blurted out a question that must have been on his mind for some time. "How did you know a lion was inside the rock?" Somewhat surprised by the question, yet pleased with the boy's thoughtfulness, the sculptor answered, "The lion was in my heart before I chiseled him in stone. Before I took hammer and chisel to the block of marble my work was in my heart."

JUST THE RIGHT FIT

It sounds almost too simple to say, too good to be true, but obedience is the very essence of the strategy of Jesus for living. It is the secret of the easy yoke: The desire to obey and to please God comes from within through a personal relationship with God in Christ. God's law fills our minds and is written on our hearts. As the Apostle Paul said, "If anyone is in Christ, he [or she] is a new creation; the old has gone, the new has come!" (2 Corinthians 5:17). Instead of falling victim to the law of sin and death, we are empowered to obey the Law of Christ.

The incident with the rich, young ruler illustrates what Jesus had in mind. For many Americans the cost of discipleship is synonymous with Jesus' challenge to this wealthy baby boomer. How could anyone conceive of giving up as much as this man was asked to give up and call it easy? The enviable young man wants something more in addition to everything else he has. He already has health and wealth, self-esteem and success; now he wants assurance that everything is all right religiously. "Teacher, what good thing must I do to get eternal life?" His opening question was intended to show respect for Jesus, but it actually did the opposite by implying that Jesus was a consultant, an expert in the Law. This explains why Jesus took issue with him, "Why do you ask me about what is good?" Jesus was not there to give good advice. This man stood before the Lord. Although he does not yet understand, much more is at stake here than an exchange of opinions. "If you want to enter life, obey the commandments," Jesus says.

The young man replied, "Which ones?" We can sympathize with the young man's failure to grasp who Jesus was, but his follow-up question is embarrassing. His over-confidence in his own ability to obey the Law is without excuse. As Jesus lists the second half of the Ten Commandments, the young man totals his moral assets with self-satisfaction. He doesn't even flinch when Jesus says, "love your neighbor as yourself." With all the self-esteem of a self-assured high achiever, he boldly asserts, "All these I have kept. What do I still lack?" Any student of the Beatitudes could tell this man what he lacked. But Jesus answered him in terms he could understand. "If you want to be perfect, go, sell your possessions and give to the poor, and you will have treasure in heaven. Then come, follow me." The call to radical divestiture reveals the extent of the young man's insensitivity to his dependence upon God. He needed to be stripped of his successful image and religious decorum and clothed with spiritual poverty and sorrow for sin. Outward conformity to the Law, shallow interpretation and superficial application, bore no resemblance to the heart righteousness Jesus was after. Anything less would have made the strategy of Jesus impossible. Without a change of heart, the promise of the easy yoke is misleading, even cruel.

In Christ, obedience is not a duty as much as it is a privilege. The follower of Jesus is committed to a Person, not an idea or an ideology. The gospel frees us to fulfill the Law through the righteousness of Christ and the example of Jesus. We are free from the law of sin and death. Therefore, by God's grace, we are free for faithfulness and obedience. Come to the Sermon on the Mount "with the legalistic mind, and it is impossible and absurd; come to it with the mind of the lover, and nothing else is possible." E. Stanley Jones expressed it well when he wrote, "The lover's attitude is not one of duty, but one of privilege. Here is the key to the Sermon on the Mount. We mistake it entirely if we look on it as the chart of the Christian's duty; rather it is the charter of the Christian's liberty."[9]

Clearly, it doesn't make sense to follow Jesus without His perspective on righteousness. It would be like playing soccer in sandals or baseball in swim fins. The yoke is easy and the burden light because Jesus fits the law of God to life in just the right way.

The Pharisees loosened and tightened the commandments to fit their purposes. Jesus applied the Law to fit our true needs. What Jesus said about the Sabbath was true for the entire Law. Man was not made for the Law, the Law was made for man. The working premise for the Pharisees was alienation; for Jesus it was reconciliation. Jesus brings the truth of the Law to life and the heart of the Law to obedience. No one could ever accuse Jesus of being an armchair quarterback or an ivory tower theologian. When it comes to Monday morning, the righteousness of Jesus is ready to go to work. The well-fitting easy yoke is ready for a workout.

"*D*on't suppose for a minute that I have come to demolish the Scriptures—either God's Law or the Prophets. I'm not here to demolish but to complete. I am going to put it all together, pull it all together in a vast panorama. God's Law is more real and lasting than the stars in the sky and the ground at your feet. Long after stars burn out and earth wears out, God's Law will be alive and working.

"Trivialize even the smallest item in God's Law and you will only have trivialized yourself. But take it seriously, show the way for others, and you will find honor in the Kingdom. Unless you do far better than the Pharisees in the matters of right living, you won't know the first thing about entering the kingdom."

MATTHEW 5:17-20, *THE MESSAGE*

"*Y*ou have heard that it was said to the people long ago, 'Do not murder, and anyone who murders will be subject to judgment.' But I tell you that anyone who is angry with his brother will be subject to judgment. Again, anyone who says to his brother, 'Raca,' is answerable to the Sanhedrin. But anyone who says, 'You fool!' will be in danger of the fire of hell.

"Therefore, if you are offering your gift at the altar and there remember that your brother has something against you, leave your gift there in front of the altar. First go and be reconciled to your brother; then come and offer your gift.

"Settle matters quickly with your adversary who is taking you to court. Do it while you are still with him on the way, or he may hand you over to the judge, and the judge may hand you over to the officer, and you may be thrown into prison. I tell you the truth, you will not get out until you have paid the last penny. . . .

"You have heard that it was said, 'Eye for eye, and tooth for tooth.' But I tell you, Do not resist an evil person. If someone strikes you on the right cheek, turn to him the other also. And if someone wants to sue you and take your tunic, let him have your cloak as well. If someone forces you to go one mile, go with him two miles. Give to the one who asks you, and do not turn away from the one who wants to borrow from you.

"You have heard that it was said, 'Love your neighbor and hate your enemy.' But I tell you: Love your enemies and pray for those who persecute you, that you may be sons of your Father in heaven. He causes his sun to rise on the evil and the good, and sends rain on the righteous and the unrighteous. If you love those who love you, what reward will you get? Are not even the tax collectors doing that? And if you greet only your brothers, what are you doing more than others? Do not even pagans do that? Be perfect, therefore, as your heavenly Father is perfect."

MATTHEW 5:21-26,38-48

CHAPTER SEVEN

Visible Righteousness

What does the world see in the life of the follower of Jesus? Jesus' description of beatitude-based obedience, the kind that surpasses the righteousness of the scribes and Pharisees, focuses on our relationship to others. Jesus does not lead with the spiritual disciplines, such as prayer or giving or fasting. Later He will discuss idolatry, profanity, and Sabbath keeping, but first He emphasizes visible righteousness in how we treat others.

The old Law, the Law apart from the gospel, tried to keep human animosity in check. "You have heard it said" judged murder, limited retaliation to an eye for an eye, and safeguarded neighborly love. But the new Law, inspired and empowered by the gospel, captured the essence of the law. "But I say to you" declared Jesus, practice love instead of hate, peace instead of revenge, and pray for your enemies.

A RADICAL PERSPECTIVE

Far from destroying the Law, Jesus deepens the meaning and application of the Law. "You have heard that it was said to the people long ago, 'Do not murder, and anyone who murders will be subject to judgment.' But I tell you that anyone who is angry with his brother will be subject to judgment" (Matthew 5:21).

Jesus frames the sixth commandment in an unusual way. Normally we explore the ethical limits of taking a life. We discuss abortion, euthanasia, capital punishment, and suicide. This is a controversial command in a violent culture such as ours. Murder is the leading cause of death among black teenagers and the tenth leading killer in the United States. With abortion on demand, the escalating suicide rate (especially among young people), doctor-advocated euthanasia, and drive-by shootings, there is no question that this command is relevant today.

Probably no one in the original Sermon on the Mount audience had committed murder. It is unlikely any person there would have been found guilty of murder in a court of law. In first-century Palestine, this must have been one of the most unbroken laws of all the Ten Commandments. Yet this is where Jesus begins, precisely with the commandment that everybody felt they kept and nobody felt they broke. That is, until Jesus gave His perspective on righteousness.

The Law outlawed murder; Jesus outlawed anger. Religion used the Law to set limits on human aggression; Jesus used the Law to show the full extent of love. The Law was first given to define and deal with the reality of sin and evil. The Law was given by Jesus to define and reveal the gospel of reconciliation.

The difference between the Pharisees and Jesus was the difference between laying down the law for a group of prison inmates and living the law of love in a family. In prison the goal is to keep the inmates from hurting one another. In a family the goal is to show love to one another. "Jesus goes behind the act of murder itself to declare that the anger and hatred which give rise to it, though not capable of being examined in a human court, are no less culpable in the sight of God. The continued validity of the sixth commandment is assumed, but a legalistic interpretation which restricts its application to the literal act alone is rejected."[1]

Until Jesus, no one had ever related murder to everyday insults and name-calling. In quick succession, Jesus cites three crimes covered by the commandment. It is not only a murderer who is subject to a trial, but "anyone who is angry with his brother." In fact, anyone who calls his brother an 'idiot' will stand trial before the supreme court, the Sanhedrin. More than that, anyone who says, 'You fool!' will be in danger of going to hell.

Jesus went to the heart of the matter by declaring that the sixth commandment could be violated, not only by cold-blooded murder, but inside-my-heart hate. The Pharisees were experts in the letter of the Law; Jesus focused on the spirit of the Law. Jesus countered "the common understanding that one's status before God could be determined by legalistic means."[2]

RIGHTEOUS ANGER

Nobody had ever taken anger as seriously as Jesus did. In fact it could be said that Jesus was angry with anger. If there is an anger rooted in pride, vanity, hatred, malice, and revenge, there is also an anger rooted in love, compassion, sacrifice, and righteousness. Early in Jesus' ministry, the Pharisees were looking for reasons to accuse Him. On one occasion they watched Him closely to see whether He would heal a man with a paralyzed hand on the Sabbath. Knowing their mind-set, Jesus asked them, "Which is lawful on the Sabbath: to do good or to do evil, to save life or to kill?" His question was met with silence. Mark tells us that Jesus "looked around at them in anger and, deeply distressed at their stubborn hearts, said to the man, 'Stretch out your hand.' He stretched it out, and his hand was completely restored. Then the Pharisees went out and began to plot with the Herodians how they might kill Jesus" (Mark 3:4-6).

Two completely different types of anger are revealed in this incident. One is born of hate and the other of holiness. The teachers of the Law accused Jesus of blasphemy and promoted the idea that He was demon-possessed. The crucifixion measures the full extent of their anger. Likewise, the Author of the

Law matched their accusations with His own. Ultimately, the full extent of His anger will be measured on the day of judgment.

> "Woe to you, teachers of the law and Pharisees, you hypocrites! You build tombs for the prophets and decorate the graves of the righteous. And you say, 'If we had lived in the days of our forefathers, we would not have taken part with them in shedding the blood of the prophets.' So you testify against yourselves that you are the descendants of those who murdered the prophets. Fill up, then, the measure of the sin of your forefathers!
> "You snakes! You brood of vipers! How will you escape being condemned to hell?" (Matthew 23:29-33)

The relationship between Jesus and the Pharisees is a dramatic case study in the difference between anger inspired by love and anger rooted in hate. Obviously, Jesus does not outlaw strong emotion and a passion for righteousness. What He outlaws is a vindictive, self-serving, hateful emotion that can kill the human spirit long before it takes a human life.

The difference between righteous anger and evil anger is the difference between anger based on alienation and anger based on reconciliation. I have a vivid memory of two occasions when my father was furious with me. He was, of course, angry with me many times, I am sure. But these two times stand out. It was in sixth grade when I swore at my mother. I said "damn" to her, against her, and my father exploded. His anger was pure passion. That is the only occasion I remember my father taking his belt off, which he ended up not using, but the impact was almost as real as if he had. I didn't realize at first what I realized later—that my father was not just angry about a four-letter word. He was angry at a way of life, a pattern of behavior. His concern went beyond my verbal abuse; he was against the lack of love and respect it showed. As long as I was his son I was not going to become the product of my peer group or give free expression to my depravity. That was the only night I ever remember kneeling with my father and praying for forgiveness.

I don't remember the second occasion being as spiritual. I had interested my brother in setting our car models on fire by pouring gasoline over them. The smell of burnt plastic must have traveled further than we thought, because my father came out to the garage to check on the odor. He caught us in the act; uncapped gasoline can and matches in hand. Once again I saw his anger. At first I thought it was no big deal, but that is why he was so angry. I pictured a little mischief. He pictured my brother and me in a burn treatment ward. Before the afternoon was over I had gotten the picture; now I can't look at a red gasoline can without thinking of that incident and my father.

As I look back on it, the intensity of my father's anger seems right and good. Very clearly it was anger against me that was prompted by love for me. There were times that I anticipated my father's anger only to be surprised by its absence (but not disappointed). For example, I had trouble figuring out why my father did not get more upset when I broke windows playing catch. Nor do I ever remember his getting mad when I made stupid plays in baseball, even though other dads seemed so agitated with their sons. Then there was the time when I was helping him nail drywall. He had spent thirty minutes cutting and fitting a large intricate piece. He put it up with a couple of nails and asked me to finish nailing it in place. Two minutes later, in the process of trying to extract a nail I had bent, I punched a sizable hole in the sheet of drywall. He took the damaged drywall off and repeated the whole process without even a word of reproof.

My purpose here is not to paint a perfect picture of my father. Everyone in the family remembers when Dad got so angry he slammed his hand down on the kitchen counter and broke his hand. Nevertheless, I was far more concerned about disappointing my father than I ever was fearful about his anger.

Obedience in our household was based on love, not alienation. It wasn't that I was afraid to go against my father; it just didn't make any sense. I didn't find my relationship with my father stifling or confining. On the contrary, it was liberating.

Jesus is not interested in diffusing or diverting evil anger. I was distraught one night coming home near midnight from a terrible church board meeting. I had been criticized up and down by a board member who was giving every indication that he wasn't going to let up until I quit. Driving along in this state of anger and tears, I punched the steering wheel so hard that the horn stuck. There I was driving down our street with my horn blasting full volume, waking up the neighborhood. My neighbor got out of bed and rushed outside to see what was wrong. After trying in vain to pull the fuse for the horn, we ended up cutting the wires. The good news in this story is that I forgot about the church board member (at least until morning). But this is not what Jesus had in mind when He commanded us to deal with anger.

RECONCILIATION BALANCED WITH INTEGRITY

Jesus wants to transform our anger by replacing the law of alienation with the law of reconciliation. Instead of a five or ten step formula for dealing with anger, Jesus offers a new perspective with two parables (Matthew 5:24-26). One story is drawn from the worship center, the other from the workplace. One concerns a brother, the other an adversary. The lesson is basically the same in both vignettes: *Do everything in your power to bring about reconciliation.* Do not even use worship as an excuse for prolonging alienation. If you rely on the legal system to settle matters, you might end up losing everything. Those who follow Jesus must take the initiative in restoring broken relationships.

In the middle of every human relationship, whether with a brother in Christ or an enemy, Jesus plants the cross. We are commanded to look at all conflict situations from the foot of the cross. The gospel enables us to enter into alienation and animosity with the assurance that good will overcome evil.

Paul offers an excellent commentary on reconciliation when he says,

> Love must be sincere. Hate what is evil; cling to what is good. Be devoted to one another in brotherly love. . . . Bless those who persecute you; bless and do not curse. . . . Do not repay anyone evil for evil. Be careful to do what is right in the eyes of everybody. If it is possible, as far as it depends on you, live at peace with everyone. Do not take revenge, my friends, but leave room for God's wrath, for it is written: "It is mine to avenge; I will repay," says the Lord. On the contrary: "If your enemy is hungry, feed him; if he is thirsty, give him something to drink. In doing this, you will heap burning coals on his head." Do not be overcome by evil, but overcome evil with good. (Romans 12:9-10,14,17-21)

There was nothing in the words and actions of Jesus that created an unnecessary offense for the Pharisees and the teachers of the Law. If Jesus had not cleansed the temple or healed the man with the withered hand, undoubtedly He would have been more acceptable to the Pharisees, but He would not have been obedient to His Father's will. True reconciliation is never at the expense of obedience.

There are no limits to the believer's responsibility to bring about reconciliation other than those limits prescribed by reconciliation itself. Reconciliation is not capitulation. It is not a denial of the good in order to pacify evil. Peacemaking is not appeasement. It should not be confused with conflict management and conflict resolution. Reconciliation means going out of our way to bring about peace, without the loss of the integrity of Christ.

But reconciliation is not always possible. The Pharisees refused to settle out of court, so to speak. They persisted in their condemnation and persecution of Jesus. They were blinded to the truth and were not satisfied until Jesus hung on the cross. Jesus emphasizes the fact that His followers will be persecuted. "Blessed are those who are persecuted because of righteousness, for theirs is the kingdom of heaven." This is the one beatitude that Jesus reiterated. "Blessed are you when people insult you, persecute you, and falsely say all kinds of evil against you because of me. Rejoice and be glad, because great is your reward in heaven, for in the same way they persecuted the prophets who were before you." We should not be surprised that in spite of peacemaking efforts, some refuse to be reconciled. Like the Pharisees, they remain the adversary for reasons they believe to be honorable and noble.

BEYOND HATE TO LOVE

The follower of Jesus does not regard anyone, including the enemy and adversary, "from a worldly point of view." We have been given the ministry of reconciliation. We look at all people as those for whom Christ died (2 Corinthians 5:16-20). My sin against God is greater by far than anyone's sin against me. God has forgiven me more than I could possibly forgive others. "Bear with each other and forgive whatever grievances you may have against one another. Forgive as the Lord forgave you" (Colossians 3:13). Conflict, in all its forms, looks different from the foot of the cross.

John Perkins, in his book *A Quiet Revolution*, describes the night he was brutally beaten by the police in Brandon, Mississippi. He had participated in a nonviolent civil rights march earlier in the day and had been arrested. He writes:

During my night in the jail at Brandon, God began something new in my life. In the midst of the crowded, noisy jailhouse, between the stomping and the black-jacking that we received; between the moments when one of the patrolmen put his pistol to my head and pulled the trigger—"CLICK"—and when another later took a fork and bent the two middle prongs down and pushed the other two up my nose until blood came out—between the reality and the insanity, between the consciousness and the unconsciousness that would sweep across my dizzy mind, between my terror and my unwillingness to break down, between my pain and my fear, in those little snatches of thought when in some miraculous way I could at once be the spectacle and the spectator, God pushed me past hatred. Just for a little while, moments at a time.

How could I hate when there was so much to pity? How could I hate people I suddenly did not recognize, who had somehow moved past the outer limits of what it means to be human . . . ? But I don't think it was just the pity I had or the deep sickness I saw alone that pushed me past hatred. It was also the fact that I was broken. . . . The Brandon experience just might have been a way of God bringing me to the place where he could expand his love in me and extend my calling to white people as well as black people. . . . And I believe that it was in my own broken state that the depth of the sickness in those men struck home to me, and the fact that I was like them—totally depraved. I had evidence before me and in myself that every human being is bad—depraved. There's something built into all of us that makes us want to be superior. If the black man had the advantage, he'd be just as bad. So I can't hate the white man. It's a spiritual problem—black or white, we all need to be born again. . . .

The failure, the frustration, the powerlessness of my situation as a black person in the South pressed me. What it was squeezing out of me was more and more bitterness. Like a lemon—so fresh and sweet looking on the outside but hiding such a sour taste. And the bitterness just made the frustration worse.

I saw how bitterness could destroy me. The Spirit of God had a hold of me and wouldn't let me sidestep his justice. And his justice said that I was just as sinful as those who beat me. But I knew that God's justice is seasoned with forgiveness. Forgiveness is what makes his justice redemptive. Forgiveness! That was the key. And somehow, God's forgiveness for me was tied up in my forgiveness of those who hurt me.

"For if you forgive men when they sin against you, your heavenly Father will also forgive you. But if you do not forgive men their sins, your Father will not forgive your sins" (Matthew 6:14-15).

We were right. . . . But now God was saying, "Being right is not enough. You must also be forgiving." Reconciliation is so difficult because the damage is so deep.[3]

John Perkins learned the power of the easy yoke. He took what was designed to destroy him and let the gospel of Jesus Christ transform him from bitterness to forgiveness. He gave up fighting the world on its own terms. He moved beyond hate to love. He couldn't hate because there was too much to pity. He moved beyond alienation to reconciliation. There was too much to forgive to be embittered. He moved from the bondage of guilt and blame to the easy yoke of Jesus. Ask yourself, which is harder, love or hate? Which is more fulfilling, revenge or forgiveness? Which is better, reconciliation or retaliation?

The strategy of Jesus for living lifts the burden and lightens the load by replacing a natural propensity toward animosity with a spiritual bent toward forgiveness and love. Behavior consistent with the easy yoke tackles anger as the first order of business. One of the blessings of being able to mourn for our sins and receive the forgiveness of Christ is the transformation of our anger. One of the benefits of Jesus-style meekness is the power of God to love our enemies. In Christ we have the grace-filled capacity to love instead of hate.

"You're familiar with the command to the ancients, 'Do not murder.' I'm telling you that anyone who is so much as angry with a brother or sister is guilty of murder. Carelessly call a brother 'idiot!' and you just might find yourself hauled into court. Thoughtlessly yell 'stupid!' at a sister and you are on the brink of hellfire. The simple moral fact is that words kill.

"This is how I want you to conduct yourself in these matters. If you enter your place of worship and, about to make an offering, you suddenly remember a grudge a friend has against you, abandon your offering, leave immediately, go to this friend and make things right. Then and only then, come back and work things out with God.

"Or say you're out on the street and an old enemy accosts you. Don't lose a minute. Make the first move; make things right with him. After all, if you leave the first move to him, knowing his track record, you're likely to end up in court, maybe even jail. If that happens, you won't get out without a stiff fine. . . .

"Here's another old saying that deserves a second look: 'Eye for eye, tooth for tooth.' Is that going to get us anywhere? Here's what I propose: 'Don't hit back at all.' If someone strikes you, stand there and take it. If someone drags you into court and sues for the shirt off your back, giftwrap your best coat and make a present of it. And if someone takes unfair advantage of you, use the occasion to practice the servant life. No more tit-for-tat stuff. Live generously.

"You're familiar with the old written law, 'Love your friend,' and its unwritten companion, 'Hate your enemy.' I'm challenging that. I'm telling you to love your enemies. Let them bring out the best in you, not the worst. When someone gives you a hard time, respond with the energies of prayer, for then you are working out of your true selves, your God-created selves. This is what God does. He give his best—the sun to warm and the rain to nourish—to everyone, regardless: the good and bad, the nice and nasty. If all you do is love the lovable, do you expect a bonus? Anybody can do that. If you simply say hello to those who greet you, do you expect a medal? Any run-of-the-mill sinner does that.

"In a word, what I'm saying is, *Grow up.* You're kingdom subjects. Now live like it. Live out your God-created identity. Live generously and graciously toward others, the way God lives toward you."

MATTHEW 5:21-26,38-48, *THE MESSAGE*

• •

"You have heard that it was said, 'Do not commit adultery.' But I tell you that anyone who looks at a woman lustfully has already committed adultery with her in his heart. If your right eye causes you to sin, gouge it out and throw it away. It is better for you to lose one part of your body than for your whole body to be thrown into hell. And if your right hand causes you to sin, cut it off and throw it away. It is better for you to lose one part of your body than for your whole body to go into hell.

"It has been said, 'Anyone who divorces his wife must give her a certificate of divorce.' But I tell you that anyone who divorces his wife, except for marital unfaithfulness, causes her to become an adulteress, and anyone who marries the divorced woman commits adultery."

MATTHEW 5:27-32

CHAPTER EIGHT

Jesus on Sex

A popular ad for a cruise ship begins "If they could see you now." Apart from the song and dance and all that frolicking on the fun ship, Jesus had the same idea. What do people see when you "let your light shine"? Evidently there is a built-in human desire to either entice or edify, entrap or enrich. In the extreme it is Madonna, the apparent personification of lust, versus Mary the mother of Christ, the first disciple. It boils down to self-generated human envy or soul-transforming glory to God.

The ad suggests there is something in human nature that likes generating a little envy in the other guy. The command of Jesus points us in the opposite direction: "Let your light shine before people that they may see your good works and glorify your Father in heaven." If this sounds flat and unappealing, it's because lust competes with love. The razzle-dazzle of a daily Mardi Gras is more entertaining than the quiet rhythms of husband and wife, parent and child, sister and brother. Life has shifted from home and neighborhood to an MTV set. It is desirable to lust for and to be lusted over. Lust may not be the worst sin, but a good case can be made for it being the most popular.

In *The Bonfire of the Vanities*, Tom Wolfe's lead character, Sherman McCoy, says to himself as he walks down Fifth Avenue:

It was in the air! It was a wave! Everywhere!
Inescapable . . . ! Sex . . . ! There for the taking . . . ! It
walked down the street, as bold as you please . . . ! It
was splashed all over the shops! If you are young and
halfway alive, what chance did you have . . . ? Who could
remain monogamous with this, this, this tidal wave of
concupiscence rolling across the world . . . ? You can't
dodge snowflakes, and this was a blizzard! He had
merely been caught at it, that was all, or halfway caught
at it. It meant nothing. It had no moral dimension. It
was nothing more than getting soaking wet.[1]

Author Tim Stafford writes, "Today any one of us encoun-
ters sexual stimulation many times a day, often from someone
whose very existence is the figment of an advertising director's imagination. We live in a constant bath of depersonalized,
imaginary, highly provocative sexuality. To the modern person,
this seems normal; he is barely aware of it."[2] When it comes to
being in the world but not of the world there may be no more
difficult battleground than sexuality.

The church is often criticized for being too preoccupied
with sexual sins. Many argue that Christians give a dispropor-
tionate emphasis to sexual sins. They neglect the sins of hate,
gossip, and revenge and equate immorality simply with sexual
immorality. In some cases this is certainly true, but sexual
issues are such a fundamental part of our culture that any dis-
agreement with our culture on this subject is bound to draw
attention. The fact that Jesus spoke so seriously about lust and
adultery can hardly be misconstrued as a preoccupation. It
would be nice if sexual morality were a peripheral issue, but it
is not. It is part of our core being, related closely to personal
identity, relationships, and family.

For the most part, our culture pretends to take a light-
hearted approach to sex. But the laughter is only on the surface. It is far more than a pastime; it is a chief passion. As C. S.
Lewis wrote, "All my life a ludicrous and portentous solem-

nization of sex has been going on."[3] If Jesus said, in the course of a press conference, "Money is the root of all evil," the next question would be, "What about sex?"

Judging from today's media, adultery is to adults what infancy is to infants. Patterson and Kim in *The Day America Told the Truth*, report, "Almost one-third of all married Americans (31%) have had or are now having an affair. This isn't a number from Hollywood or New York City. It's the national average for adultery. . . . Today the majority of Americans (62%) think that there's nothing morally wrong with the affairs they're having. Once again, we hear the killer rationalization that 'everybody else does it too.' . . . Adultery in contemporary America is as likely to occur in Manhattan, Kansas, as it is in Manhattan, New York."[4]

All this is to say that the mind-set of the people Jesus addressed is different from today's audience. When it came to sexual sin, virtually everyone, especially the Pharisees, felt they had obeyed to the letter of the Law. The stability of the family and respect for the moral law kept promiscuity at bay.

The Pharisees "gave a conveniently narrow definition of sexual sin and a conveniently broad definition of sexual purity."[5] People today have narrowed the definition of sexual sin even further to exclude fornication, adultery, and homosexual practice. If such acts, let alone the desire, are no longer sinful, then Jesus really is a voice in the wilderness.

Lust has become a rite of passage in the modern world. When I was thirteen, I attended my best friend's *Bar mitzvah*. His father ran a local casino-cabaret that was identified by most people in town as an evil place. Nevertheless, that did not distract from our friendship. Ron's home life and his father's work seemed to be in different worlds. It was a privilege being one of the few non-Jewish people at the service. The rabbi, with his long beard and deep voice, solemnly reading from the Torah, dedicated Ron as a son of the Law. After the reception all the relatives went back to Ron's house and all the guys, his brother, cousins, and myself, went up to Ron's room to talk. His older brother had in mind a different initiation. He brought from his room literally stacks of *Playboy* and similar magazines and strewed them on the floor, releasing a kind of feeding frenzy among the boys. I left dismayed and walked home alone. That day manliness was defined by the law and lust.

DESIRE OR LUST?
The Bible distinguishes between sexual desire and sexual lust; the former is rooted in God's creation, the latter in human depravity. Author Paul Mickey offers a helpful definition:

> Lust is any excessive desire, any uncontrollable urge for immediate gratification. . . . Lust may involve a craving for food, alcohol, sports, new fashions, success, sex. . . . Lust of any type is dangerous because it is self-centered, mechanistic, inflexible, and insensitive to the needs of others. . . . Lust is selfish, insensitive, self-gratification. Lust is a powerful force that is rooted deeply in our selfish, rebellious nature.[6]

Sexual desire is healthy; sexual lust is unhealthy. The Greek word for lust combines both sexual desire and possession. There is a difference between looking and lusting, appreciating and devouring, and the line between them is crossed in the heart. Lust is not simply treating the opposite sex as a sex object. That is too narrow a definition. It is using the other person to feed one's sexual appetite. Lust divorces love, spurns care, denies communion, and disregards commitment. The Bible underscores the goodness of sexual desire and the badness of sexual lust. Sexual intimacy was meant to be encouraged and protected in the personal, public, sacred commitment of marriage. Lust is a dehumanizing, depersonalizing drive to indulge the sexual appetite.

It is not uncommon for lust to invoke a complex sequence of rationalization such as, "No one gets hurt in a private sexual fantasy world. As long as I don't have an affair, I'm not hurting anyone." Or, "Pornography is for private 'entertainment.'" "It's just a normal curiosity." Or, "My sex drive is too strong to be controlled according to biblical standards." Or, "If I hadn't had such a sexually repressed childhood, or a distant parent, or low self-esteem, then maybe I wouldn't have such a strong sex drive."[7]

Sexual desire can be overwhelmed by sexual lust. In *When Society Becomes an Addict*, psychologist Anne Wilson Schaef writes, "The system in which we live is an addictive system. . . . Sex has been increasingly identified as an addictive process. More and more people seem to be using sex not as a means of relating but as a way of getting a fix. . . . When a sex addict gets a fix, it serves the same purpose as a drink or a drug, and the personality dynamics that develop are essentially the same."[8]

Throughout history, Christians have been tempted to equate sexual desire with sexual lust and impose a standard on discipleship Jesus never intended. The great fourth-century church father, Augustine, convinced many that sex, even within the bonds of marriage, was a necessary evil. The goal of the believer was to obey God and procreate the human race with as little sexual desire as possible. To have sex without passion was the ideal. Confusion over desire and lust is behind the requirement for a celibate priesthood. Sexual desire becomes tainted with the judgment reserved for lust. This is one area where religion has failed by imposing on the followers of Jesus a yoke of its own making. This is an example of how the easy yoke of Jesus has been transformed into a heavy yoke. Paul warned Timothy about those who confuse self-denial with self-negation and reject what God has created: "They forbid people to marry and order them to abstain from certain foods, which God created to be received with thanksgiving by those who believe and who know the truth. For everything God created is good, and nothing is to be rejected if it is received with thanksgiving, because it is consecrated by the word of God and prayer" (1 Timothy 4:3-5).

A RIVAL GOD

Today's idolatrous fixation with sex is reminiscent of ancient fertility cults. The human quest for transcendence and meaning focuses on sexual salvation. Sex is the sacrament in the new age. Tim Stafford observes,

> Sex as savior has an astonishing quality to it. C. S. Lewis caught it when he wrote, "You can get a large audience together for a striptease act—that is, to watch a girl undress on a stage. Now suppose you came to a country where you could fill a theater by simply bringing a covered plate on to the stage and then slowly lifting the cover so as to let every one see, just before the lights went out, that it contained a mutton chop or a piece of bacon. . . ." Such behavior would show, Lewis said, that something had gone wrong with people's appetite for food. But there is a subtler implication. It would be strange for people to crowd into a room to see a piece of bacon uncovered, but perhaps no stranger than what one sees in any Christian church when people take Communion, lovingly [reverently] holding and distributing tiny bits of bread and drops of wine. In religion, simple things become infused with a greater meaning. They gain a fascination and an emotional importance far beyond their practical function. So it is with sex in our time: It has become a sacrament.[9]

Jesus does not treat sex lightly. He recognizes that lust is a rival god that may reign in the soul long before it makes its epiphany in outward actions. What is so radical about Jesus' redemptive approach is that He deals with the overt act by attacking the covert desire. Obedience is not measured in a court of law, but in the sight of God. God alone can see the heart. No one can legislate thoughts or feelings; they lie outside the domain of human judgment, but they do not lie outside the domain of God's judgment. In that sense there are no such things as private thoughts and passions. Lust not only possesses the object of passion, first in mind, then in body, but comes between us and God. Lust messes up both human relationships and communion with God.

Lust-free love is not based on conquest, but commitment. "Jesus' demand calls for nothing less than a totally wholesome relationship between man and woman in which evil itself is no longer predominant. . . . The root of the problem lies within one's person, one's relationship with others. Jesus' demand therefore presupposes a new starting point in man-woman relationships."[10] Sexual lust does not fit in the new relationships created by Christ Jesus.

OVERCOMING LUST WITH LOVE

Jesus calls for drastic measures to avoid total annihilation.[11] Is sex such a core issue that it is crucial to my eternal destiny? Jesus thought so and the measures suggested for saving oneself are extreme. Can you imagine what would happen if someone sought counseling for sexual lust and they were told to gouge out their eye or cut off their hand?! This sounds like the ultimate behavior modification.

Note that Jesus did not suggest castration. Ironically some in the early church, notably Origen of Alexandria, tried to take Jesus literally on this point and castrated themselves. Tragically, as their barbaric practice illustrates, they missed the point. Jesus was not advising self-mutilation, but self-mortification. The believer is disabled, not literally, but volitionally, for the sake of the gospel. It is as if he had no eyes to see what he should not see or hands to do what he should not do. A whole new order of human relationships makes seducing and being seduced unthinkable.

Don't look! Behave as if you had actually plucked out your eyes and flung them away, and were now blind and so could not see the objects which previously caused you to sin. . . . Don't do it! Don't go! Behave as if you had actually cut off your hands and feet, and had flung them away, and were now crippled and so could not do the things or visit the places which previously caused you to sin. That is the meaning of mortification.[12]

St. Paul captured the difference between mortification and mutilation when he wrote, "I have been crucified with Christ and I no longer live, but Christ lives in me. The life I live in the body, I live by faith in the Son of God, who loved me and gave himself for me" (Galatians 2:20). Dealing with lust is not only a physical and psychological issue, but a spiritual issue. Freud thought that God was a substitute for sex, but it is the other way around, sex has become a substitute for God. "The passionate gravity of the soul is meant for God. When the true God comes, the false gods go. To conquer lust, forget about lust and love God."[13]

PROTECTING OUR LONGINGS

Forgetting about lust may be about as easy as plucking your eye out or cutting your hand off, but no one said it was going to be easy to "take captive every thought to make it obedient to Christ" (2 Corinthians 10:5). We need some practical help and a few suggestions may be in order.

We would not think of exposing ourselves to dangerous levels of radiation for fear that we might get cancer. However, it may be even more important to limit our exposure to sexual stimulation. We are inundated by sexual material everywhere, on television, at work, in books and movies.

When I first came to San Diego I discovered the heavy breathing cable television station. You know the one that is seductively scrambled. At first it takes you aback that people actually do that stuff in front of cameras. I didn't like the idea that every time I turned on the TV the sex station was only a button press away. It was too tempting to flip to the channel and see what kind of weird thing they were doing now. So we asked the cable company to block it, not for the kids, but for me.

Guarding our hearts and minds in Christ Jesus need not be negative. There is so much that we can see and handle and do that enriches and strengthens. "Whatever is true, whatever is noble, whatever is right, whatever is pure, whatever is lovely, whatever is admirable—if anything is excellent or praise-worthy—think about such things. . . . And the God of peace will be with you" (Philippians 4:8-9).

Walter Wangerin encourages us to form a "self-conscious distant early warning line" within the soul.[14] It is healthy to make some up-front determinations. Like Job when he explained to God, "I made a covenant with my eyes not to look lustfully at a girl" (31:1). Or Joseph, who determined to resist being seduced by Potiphar's wife: "And though she spoke to Joseph day after day, he refused to go to bed with her or even be with her" (Genesis 39:10).

At Niagara Falls, you are able to walk out to the very edge of the precipice. On the Canadian side of Horseshoe Falls, the only thing separating you from the torrent is a waist-high rail-ing. A short jump and anyone could plunge over the falls to his death. I am not suicidal, but I have always found that spot scary. Right at the edge it just seems too easy to fall over the Falls.

Sexual immorality "is never a sudden, spontaneous, and totally unexpected act. It is always preceded by a longer drama, at the beginning of which you are not helpless."[15] It is impor-tant that we be aware of the incremental steps in moral decision-making. Being seduced by lust is a process. The fur-ther we go in that process the closer we get to the precipice. Walter Wangerin's counsel is important:

> When a desire is born in us, we have a choice. When it exists still in its infancy, we have a choice. We can care-fully refuse its existence altogether, since it needs our complicity to exist. We can dread it from the very begin-ning, naming it straightway as a parasite that intends no good for us. Or else we can attend to it, think about it, fantasize it into a greater existence—feed it! We can feed our sexual thoughts with pictures, books, videos,

and a wandering eye at work. But if we do the latter, if we give it attention in our souls, soon we will be giving it our souls. We've lost free will and the opportunity to choose. The desire itself overpowers us, commanding action, demanding satisfaction. The only choice left, since we've been enslaved by a passion, is how we might justify the sin.[16]

Overcoming lust with love is not only a personal challenge but a household of faith challenge. There is a need for families and churches, youth groups and students to form a Christian counterculture. It is not enough for the church to stand against sexual immorality. The household of faith ought "to provide another world, a society that strengthens, encourages, teaches, and models a distinctive way of living sexually. The church ought to be a sexual counterculture."[17]

It has never been more important for the church to teach clearly and strongly the Word of God on sexual morality. Nor has the need ever been greater to nurture loving, faithful, monogamous marriages and model healthy, holy singleness. The day of vague platitudes is over. We have so much more to say to teenagers than "Be careful." The church cannot remain faithful to Christ by being a "blessing machine," sprinkling holy water on secular relationships. We have a responsibility to build up the Body of Christ, not jeopardize it by being seduced by the world.

I will say it again: The gospel of reconciliation is behind every statement, warning, and demand in the Sermon on the Mount. Jesus offers the good news that there is forgiveness in His cross and resurrection. There is a power greater than sexual lust that liberates the life from the bondage of sin and death. It is not too late to receive the benediction of Jesus: "Blessed are the pure in heart, for they will see God."

At first the cost of discipleship may appear overwhelming, especially with respect to sexual purity. In time, however, the believer discovers the value of the easy yoke. Purity instead of lust lightens the load and lifts the burden. Lust is a cancer that eats away at the soul and destroys relationships. From the world's perspective, the follower of Jesus may suffer a disability, but that limitation is our liberation; that self-denial our self-fulfillment. Love, not lust, fulfills sexual desire.

If they could see you now, would your light so shine before others that they would see your good deeds and glorify your Father in Heaven? Would people be enticed or edified? Under the easy yoke we move from lust to love, and love is a far lighter load to bear than lust.

"*Y*ou know the next commandment pretty well, too: 'Don't go to bed with another's spouse.' But don't think you've preserved your virtue simply by staying out of bed. Your heart can be corrupted by lust even quicker than your body. Those leering looks you think nobody notices—they also corrupt.

"Let's not pretend this is easier than it really is. If you want to live a morally pure life, here's what you have to do: You have to blind your right eye the moment you catch it in a lustful leer. You have to choose to live one-eyed or be dumped on a moral trash pile. And you have to chop off your right hand the moment you notice it raised threateningly. Better a bloody stump than your entire being discarded for good in the dump.

"Remember the Scripture that says, 'Whoever divorces his wife, let him do it legally, giving her divorce papers and her legal rights'? Too many of you are using that as a cover for selfishness and whim, pretending to be righteous just because you are 'legal.' Please, no more pretending. If you divorce your wife, you're responsible for making her an adulteress (unless she has already made herself that by sexual promiscuity). And if you marry such a divorced adulteress, you're automatically an adulterer yourself. You can't use legal cover to mask a moral failure."

MATTHEW 5:27-32, *THE MESSAGE*

"Again, you have heard that it was said to the people long ago, 'Do not break your oath, but keep the oaths you have made to the Lord.' But I tell you, Do not swear at all: either by heaven, for it is God's throne; or by the earth, for it is his footstool; or by Jerusalem, for it is the city of the Great King. And do not swear by your head, for you cannot make even one hair white or black. Simply let your 'Yes' be 'Yes,' and your 'No,' 'No'; anything beyond this comes from the evil one."

MATTHEW 5:33-37

CHAPTER NINE

Simple Honesty

Jesus' revolutionary strategy for living, "You have heard it said . . . but I say to you," highlights a way of life that is antithetical to both religious and secular thinking. Yet He follows it with an even more shocking statement: "Be perfect, therefore, as your heavenly Father is perfect" (Matthew 5:48). At this point you might feel like saying: "Yeah, right! I find it hard to get out of bed on Sunday morning and you're saying, 'Be perfect like God.' Do you honestly mean to say that this is what the easy yoke, promised by Jesus, is all about? This description of what it means to follow Jesus is not only difficult, it's impossible."

A follower of Jesus needs to understand that becoming like our heavenly Father has much more to do with simple honesty and truthfulness than with heroic accomplishments. Living out our God-created identity in love and honesty may run against the grain of our depravity, but it fits well with who we really want to be and what the world longs to see.

WINSOME EVANGELISM

I attended a theology conference entitled, "Christian Apologetics in a Postmodern World." The theologians struggled with how to tell people about Jesus and commend His gospel to a world that increasingly claims human knowledge, ethics, and language have no other reality than human invention. How we think, what we value, and the language we use to communicate have no other basis than the Self. All talk is merely rhetoric and the rhetoric has no connection with reality. Reality itself is a myth. There is no such thing as truth, only opinion, preference, and a personal point of view.

The modern mind-set is skeptical; the mood cynical; every claim must be debunked and every value exposed. Intellectual disciplines, like philosophy, psychology, and sociology are nothing more than a disposable by-product of human activity. The imperial Self is the master of the universe. This century's Copernican revolution places all that is or was or ever will be in orbit around the Self. "Freedom is to choose," declares the culture. But Jesus says, "If you hold to my teaching, you are really my disciples. Then you will know the truth and the truth will make you free."

The keynote speaker was David Wells, author of the widely read work, *No Place for Truth, Or Whatever Happened to Evangelical Theology?* After retelling the woes of modernity, Professor Wells was asked: "Given all that you've said, what should we do?" "What we need to do," Wells prescribed, "is emphasize the holiness of God." The follow-up question and ensuing discussion centered on how to do this. As one person said, "When you speak of holiness I think of the uptight, narrow-minded, fundamentalist, sectarian church I grew up in. My church prided itself on remaining small and pure." Another participant asked, "How do we present the awesome, victorious, fulfilling holiness of God in a compelling and convincing way?" There is no easy answer to this question, but this is where I believe the invitation of the easy yoke and the instruction of the Sermon on the Mount is invaluable to the follower of Jesus.

The compelling splendor of God's holy righteousness is revealed in the disciples of Jesus being loving as their heavenly Father is loving; pure as their heavenly Father is pure; faithful as their heavenly Father is faithful; truthful as their heavenly Father is truthful; forgiving as their heavenly Father is forgiving. The culture may equate being holy with being "holier than thou," but Jesus did not. He equated holiness with a radical new approach to relationships—reconciliation rather than alienation.

The meaning of discipleship is not expressed in a carefully constructed apologetic or in a philosophical world view, but in the rough and tumble of everyday relationships. This is where the world was meant to see the holiness of God. Simple honesty will do more for the cause of Christ than lectures in epistemology arguing for the nature of truth. For those who have given up on truth in principle, truthful people are the only way they may see the truth.

When it comes to evangelism, believers feel intimidated, fearing they will not have the right words to defend their faith. Evangelicalism's quick-witted, answer-for-everything apologists may have done more harm than good by unintentionally implying that ordinary believers are not prepared "to give an answer to everyone who asks you to give the reason for the hope that you have" (1 Peter 3:15). But evangelism does not depend on a memory bank of facts and verses or clever responses to trick questions.

William Willimon, dean of the chapel and professor of Christian ministry at Duke University, shares the story of one student's approach. Converted in his senior year of high school, this fresh, eager Christian went to hear evangelical activist Dr. Tony Campolo speak. He responded to Campolo's invitation to sign up for inner-city ministry in Philadelphia. He told his story to Professor Willimon:

> Well, in mid-June, I met about a hundred other kids in a Baptist church in Philadelphia. We had about an hour of church, we were really worked up, all enthusiastic and ready to go. Dr. Campolo then preached for about an hour, and when he finished, people were shouting, standing on the pews clapping. It was great.

"Okay, gang, are you ready to go out there and tell 'em about Jesus?" he asked. "Yeah, let's go," we shouted back.

"Get on the bus!" Tony shouted. So we spilled out of the church and onto the bus. We were singing, clapping. But then we began to drive deeper into the depths of the city. We weren't in a great neighborhood when we started riding, but it got worse. Gradually we stopped singing, and everybody, all of us college kids, were just staring out the windows. We were scared.

Then the bus pulled up before one of the worst-looking housing projects in Philadelphia. Tony jumped on the bus and said, "All right gang, get out there and tell 'em about Jesus. I'll be back at five o'clock."

We made our hesitant way off the bus, stood there on the corner and had prayer, then we spread out. I walked down the sidewalk and stopped before a huge tenement house. I gulped, said a prayer, and ventured inside. There was a terrible odor. Windows were out. No lights in the hall. I walked up one flight of stairs toward the door where I heard a baby crying. I knocked on the door.

"Who is it?" said a loud voice inside. Then the door was cracked open and a woman holding a naked baby peered out at me. "What you want?" she asked in a harsh, mean voice.

I told her that I wanted to tell her about Jesus. With that, she swung the door open and began cursing me. She cursed me all the way down the hall, down the flight of steps, out to the sidewalk.

I felt terrible. "Look at me," I said to myself. "Some Mr. Christian I am. How in the world could somebody like me think that I could tell about Jesus?"

I sat down on the curb and cried. Then I looked up and noticed a store on the corner, windows all boarded up, bars over the door. I went to the store, walked in, looked around. Then I remembered. The baby had no diapers. The mother was smoking. I bought a box of disposable diapers and a pack of cigarettes.

I walked back to the tenement house, said a prayer, walked in, walked up the flight of stairs, gulped, stood before the door, and knocked.

"Who is it?" said the voice inside. When she opened the door, I slid that box of diapers and those cigarettes in. She looked at them, looked at me, and said, "Come in."

I stepped into the dingy apartment.

"Sit down," she commanded.

I sat down on the old sofa and began to play with the baby. I put a diaper on the baby, even though I have never put one on before. When the woman offered me a cigarette, even though I don't smoke, I smoked. I stayed there all afternoon, talking, playing with the baby, listening to the woman.

About four o'clock, the woman looked at me and said, "Let me ask you something. What's a nice college boy like you doing in a place like this?"

So I told her everything I knew about Jesus. It took me about five minutes. Then she said, "Pray for me and my baby that we can make it out of here alive."

And I prayed.[1]

This true story illustrates the impact of humility and honesty—two essential qualities for sharing Christ with people. In a survival of the fittest world, the holiness of God is both disarming and redemptive. The challenge to be perfect as your heavenly Father is perfect finds fulfillment in the practical, this-worldly wholeness and holiness of the Sermon on the Mount.

It bears repeating, simple honesty will do more for evangelism than any impressive apologetic. E. Stanley Jones, a missionary to India early in this century, recounts an incident in which a learned apologist embarrassed his opponent.

I once listened to a noted Christian controversialist on a debate with an Arya Samajist. He asked the Arya a question in long, Arabic phrases which the Arya was endeavoring to answer. When he was through, the Christian arose in his large-proportioned dignity and floored his opponent with this statement: "If you can prove that you even understood my question, let alone answering it, I will become an Arya." The crowd applauded; but I think Jesus would have wept over the travesty of religion, for they were each trying to gain victory by mental gymnastics and complicated speech instead of trying to find truth by open simplicity.[2]

Believers seem to have a natural proclivity to turn holiness into religiosity and evangelism into argumentative apologetics. Jesus chose a different approach—simple, straightforward honesty.

PLAIN TRUTH

Our society doesn't expect the plain truth anymore. "Deceit is almost a lifestyle," writes ethicist Lewis Smedes. "In our society the plain truth often puts one at a distinct disadvantage."[3] In the PBS special *The Truth about Lying*, Bill Moyers reported that the seven astronauts who died in the Challenger space shuttle disaster were never told of the dangers of launching in cold temperatures. A behind-the-scenes debate raged between the engineers of Morton Thiokol on one side and the company's managers and NASA on the other. To bolster NASA's public image, information about the dangers of the launch was suppressed. When Morton Thiokol's engineers refused to give the go-ahead, they were removed from the decision-making process. In spite of their serious objections, the Challenger was launched and millions witnessed the disastrous consequences. Once the private debate became public, the world learned of NASA's deception and cover-up.

Intentional deception is now commonplace in political

communication. Truth is carefully selected and filtered to convey to the public what politicians want the public to think. Truth is no longer simply told, it is "managed." And some politicians have a knack for making their untruthfulness seem so straight and true. When a politician says the word *frankly*, he or she is almost never being frank.

Public communication, Moyers says, has become the art of deception. President Lyndon Johnson deceived the American people on the true nature of the conflict in Vietnam. He refused to tell America the cost of mobilizing our armed forces out of fear that his plans for "The Great Society" would be jeopardized. Congress and the American people did not learn the truth about Watergate and the Iran-contra affair until layers upon layers of deception had been scraped away.

What is true in politics is also true in business. Here too, the truth is hedged, dodged, and trimmed. Marketplace savvy usually means that people know how to finesse the truth to their own advantage. An implied yes one day can be easily switched to a no the next if it serves self-interest. Yesterday's "strategic leak" becomes today's "unfounded rumor." Executives put a spin on the facts and a style of candor becomes more important than the truth itself. A manager convinces a board of directors of his opinion and then reports to his employees that the board is pushing him to make drastic cuts. Unnamed sources are used to bolster one's own slant on the truth.

Machiavelli wrote in 1513 in *The Prince* that "a prince who wishes to retain his power must learn *not* to be good, and to use, or not to use, that ability according to necessity."[4]

Everyone realizes how laudable it is for a prince to keep his word and to live by honesty, not cunning. Nevertheless, we see from contemporary experience that those princes who have done great deeds have held their word in little esteem; they have known how to bewilder men's wits through cunning, and in the end have gotten the better of those who relied on sincerity.[5]

Machiavelli goes on to describe the art of deception: "A

good ruler must not only be like the lion, but must also learn to be like the fox. A wise ruler cannot and should not respect his word, when such respect works to his disadvantage and when the reasons for which he made his promise no longer exist. . . . A prince has never failed to have legitimate reasons for whitewashing his failure to respect his word. . . . But a prince must know how to whitewash these attributes (of the fox) perfectly, to be a liar and a hypocrite."[6]

The Pentagon has a saying: "The truth is so precious it needs to be protected by a bodyguard of lies." But the arsenal of truthlessness is far greater than the bold-faced lie. Deceit and deception, manipulation and misrepresentation, slanting and selecting, gossip and rumor make war against the truth. When the truth is concealed, managed, stroked, or spiritualized, what chance does simple honesty have? This is not a new problem created by the modern political spin doctor or tabloid journalists.

THE TRUTH ABOUT TRUTHFULNESS

Apparently truth was as rare a commodity in Jesus' day as it is now. A complex system of rationalization had developed to shield people from meaning what they say and saying what they mean. Swearing an oath was akin to our written legal contract. Depending on the precise wording of the oath, they could feel good about their integrity and at the same time deny that they ever made a commitment. The law then as now provided loopholes.

Knowing the human propensity for dishonesty, the Pharisees ostensibly protected the truth by insisting on taking an oath. In a court of law, we place our hand on the Bible. "Do you swear to tell the whole truth and nothing but the truth, so help you God?" We answer, "I do." The purpose of this oath is to insist on truthfulness or suffer the consequences of perjury.

Stephen Westerholm writes in *Jesus and Scribal Authority*: "At the time of Jesus, the divine name YHWH was carefully avoided in ordinary speech to ensure that it was not taken 'in vain'; hence, various substitutes were employed in oaths. Popular usage included oaths by anything thought sacred or specially precious. But the matter did not stop there: rabbinic literature witnesses to the widespread use of the most capricious oaths to attest even trivial statements."[7]

This proliferation of oaths gave the scribes and Pharisees a distinct advantage in claiming one thing but intending something else. They could get out of a verbal commitment because they did not take the right vow, leaving those untutored in the complexities of oath-taking feeling frustrated and taken. They could make impressive public commitments before an unsuspecting audience, knowing full well they could always get out of the vow with their integrity intact, because of their precise wording of the oath. They infringed on the sovereignty of God by bolstering their claims with sanctimonious language, "but their words were the trumpets of hypocrisy."[8]

By sweeping aside all oaths Jesus was not making a case against taking an oath in a court of law or signing a contract, as some believers have concluded. He was actually doing something far more radical. He was saying in effect that our word should be true whether we are on the witness stand or the playing field. Whether we are speaking the truth "on the record" or "off the record." In other words, we don't say one thing to a person and another thing behind that person's back. Simple honesty means our word is as good over the phone as it is on a signed legal contract. Where we say it, how we say it, to whom we say it, makes no difference at all. Jesus put it bluntly: Let your "Yes" be "Yes" and your "No" be "No." "Such a demand presupposes the context of total honesty in human relationships."[9]

Genesis begins with God speaking creation into existence. God said, "Let there be. . . . And there was." This world-making Word of God creates reality. "By faith we understand that the universe was formed at God's command, so that what is seen was not made out of what was visible" (Hebrews 11:3).

The Gospel of John carries the speech of God further in

"the Word that became flesh and lived for a while among us . . . full of grace and truth." All truth be it personal or public, empirical or relational, historical or mathematical, relational or technological has its source and bearings in the creative, redemptive Word of God. This is why the speech of the disciple of the Living Word is so important. For all believers there is only one language, and that is truth. Nothing is said or could be said that will not be either affirmed or refuted by the Word of God. All speech is before the presence of God. There is no safe place for a lie and no wrong place for the truth.

The spirituality of truthfulness is foundational to the ethics of telling the truth. Dietrich Bonhoeffer wisely rooted the believer's speech in the believer's relationship with the Lord of the Cross.

> The commandment of complete truthfulness is really only another name for the totality of discipleship. Only those who follow Jesus and cleave to him are living in complete truthfulness. Such people have nothing to hide from their Lord. Their life is revealed before him, Jesus has recognized them and led them into the way of truth. . . . Only those who are in a state of truthfulness through the confession of their sin to Jesus are not ashamed to tell the truth wherever it must be told. . . . It is only because we follow Jesus that we can be genuinely truthful, for then he reveals to us our sin upon the cross. The cross is God's truth about us, and therefore it is the only power which can make us truthful. When we know the cross we are no longer afraid of the truth. We need no more oaths to confirm the truth of our utterances, for we live in the perfect truth of God.[10]

A CAREFUL WORK

The spirituality of truthfulness rooted in the Cross leads to the simplicity and solidarity of truthfulness. Liberated from manipulation and posturing, the believer experiences the blessing of simplicity. Yet Jesus meant nothing simplistic by his impera-tive, "Simply let your 'Yes' be 'Yes,' and your 'No,' be 'No.'" Saying whatever pops in your mind or venting your feelings is a poor substitute for telling the truth. "A blizzard of unconsid-ered words may be a glad release of personal emotion," but it is not "speaking the truth in love" (Ephesians 4:15).[11] Truthful-ness is not dumping on people, unloading on them without thought for accuracy or their feelings. Truthfulness requires a careful work.

There may be no greater laboratory for learning how to communicate with care than in the marriage relationship. "Truthfulness," writes Walter Wangerin, "hides nothing in lying; it neglects nothing important; it distorts nothing, either con-sciously or unconsciously; it communicates as accurate a pic-ture as possible of anything it chooses to offer, whether of the world, or of yourself, or of your spouse."[12] Wangerin continues: "Such watchfulness of talk takes work, not only to resist the impulse to keep things to yourself, but also to train yourself in choosing what to say and how to say it most effectively for the sake of your spouse. Though God gave us tongues, we are a race lazy at speech; though he gave us eyes, we are lazy in observation; and though he gave us hearts, we are inclined to be self-centered."[13]

Telling the truth, simply and carefully is a labor of love requiring two cares: "care for the topic, to get it right; and care for the person receiving your message, that she/he hear it right. That's work."[14] The reward for this simple, truth-telling lifestyle is invaluable. When a disciple's yes and no can be depended on; when her words are honest and caring, the fruit of her labor is trust and friendship, security and intimacy. The gift she receives is the solidarity of truthfulness. "Untruthfulness destroys fellowship," wrote Bonhoeffer, "but truth cuts false fel-lowship to pieces and establishes genuine brotherhood. We cannot follow Christ unless we live in revealed truth before God and man."[15]

Truthfulness, like the Word of God, is a double-edged

sword. There are two sides to simple honesty; there is a "Yes" and there is a "No." The "Yes" accepts; the "No" rejects. The disciple's language separates that which is true from that which is false. There is a decisive owning and disowning, accepting and denying. Christians can be confused on this, because some want all speech to be positive while others seem to want it all negative. Truthfulness suffers distortion in a tragic one-sidedness.

The reality of sin requires a "No," but the reality of grace requires a "Yes." The heartfelt affirmation of Christian worship and the well-informed, decisive "yes" of true commitment lead to an equally important and resolute "no." The grace of God "teaches us to say 'no' to ungodliness and worldly passions, and to live self-controlled, upright and godly lives in this present age, while we wait for the blessed hope—the glorious appearing of our great God and Savior, Jesus Christ, who gave himself for us to redeem us from all wickedness and to purify for himself a people that are his very own, eager to do what is good" (Titus 2:12-14).

Let me close this chapter by pointing out that judging from popular opinion, simple honesty places one at a distinct disadvantage in this culture. Politicians do not practice it, advertisers deny it, entrepreneurs ignore it, academics rationalize it, and entertainers joke about it. Is it any wonder then that Jesus chose it as His *modus operandi*? He laid aside *deceptive language*, refusing to say what He did not mean to say; *flattering language*, resisting the temptation to say what the other person wanted to hear; *manipulative language*, rejecting the impulse to control others; *flowery language*, choosing to communicate, rather than impress; and *misleading language*, denying the option to betray the truth.

On the contrary, He chose truth, the language that lightens the burden and gives rest for the soul. Being yoked to Jesus makes it difficult to speak any language other than the truth. "You will know the truth, and the truth will set you free" (John 8:32).

"And don't say anything you don't mean. This counsel is embedded deep in our traditions. You only make things worse when you lay down a smoke screen of pious talk, saying, 'I'll pray for you,' and never doing it, or saying, 'God be with you,' and not meaning it. You don't make your words true by embellishing them with religious lace. In making your speech sound more religious, it becomes less true. Just say 'yes' and 'no.' When you manipulate words to get your own way, you go wrong."

MATTHEW 5:33-37, *THE MESSAGE*

"*Be* careful not to do your 'acts of righteousness' before men, to be seen by them. If you do, you will have no reward from your Father in heaven.

"So when you give to the needy, do not announce it with trumpets, as the hypocrites do in the synagogues and on the streets, to be honored by men. I tell you the truth, they have received their reward in full. But when you give to the needy, do not let your left hand know what your right hand is doing, so that your giving may be in secret. Then your Father, who sees what is done in secret, will reward you.

"And when you pray, do not be like the hypocrites, for they love to pray standing in the synagogues and on the street corners to be seen by men. I tell you the truth, they have received their reward in full. But when you pray, go into your room, close the door and pray to your Father, who is unseen. Then your Father, who sees what is done in secret, will reward you. . . .

"When you fast, do not look somber as the hypocrites do, for they disfigure their faces to show men they are fasting. I tell you the truth, they have received their reward in full. But when you fast, put oil on your head and wash your face, so that it will not be obvious to men that you are fasting, but only to your Father, who is unseen; and your Father, who sees what is done in secret, will reward you."

MATTHEW 6:1-6,16-18

Hidden Righteousness

There is a popular beach on Kauai, one of the Hawaiian islands, where people go to see what is below the surface. The day we were there the skies were overcast and it was cool and rainy. Compared to other beaches the water seemed dark and uninviting. Our son, Andrew, was the first to swim out and dive below the surface. Within seconds he was yelling for us to join him, saying, "You'll never believe it! You've never seen anything like it!" And he was right. Below the surface, the coral reef was teeming with fish; all kinds of shapes, sizes, and colors. It was a whole different world, unexpected by the uninitiated.

Andrew had a terrifying experience that day. We were swimming together about fifteen feet apart when I saw his head shoot up from the water. He looked at me in absolute terror, didn't say a word, and started swimming for shore as if his life depended on it. A man swimming close to Andrew popped above the surface with the same reaction, shouting something about the biggest fish he had ever seen in his life. He took off for the shore right behind Andrew. To this day Andrew thinks he saw an eight-foot shark. No one will ever have to convince Andrew that there is a whole different world below the surface of the ocean.

No one can understand ocean life from above the surface.

To know the ocean we have to go below the surface and explore its depths. This is true in the spiritual realm as well. What's below the surface makes all the difference in the world.

BELOW THE SURFACE

Up to this point we've been examining how Jesus describes visible, public righteousness; holiness made real in the everyday, nitty-gritty world of hate and lust, manipulation and retaliation. Now we will look at what Jesus has to say about a secret, hidden righteousness. In Matthew 6 He takes us below the surface of religious appearances and explores the interior of the soul. He wants us to distinguish between the artificial and the real in our relationship with our heavenly Father.

The description Jesus gives of beatitude-based obedience and salt and light impact is based profoundly on the hidden righteousness of personal communion with God. The believer's public ethic, too, is vitally connected to personal spirituality. If the easy yoke means honesty between people, it also means integrity with our heavenly Father. The bottom line in the believer's relationship with others, "be perfect as your heavenly Father is perfect," is the first line in the believer's relationship with God.

The guiding principle for visible righteousness is clear: "Let your light shine before [people], that they may see your good deeds and praise your Father in heaven" (Matthew 5:16). What follows is a clear and contrasting warning, "Be careful not to do your 'acts of righteousness' before [people], to be seen by them. If you do, you will have no reward from your Father in heaven" (Matthew 6:1). Put side by side, the two statements seem to contradict one another.

On the one hand, Jesus is telling His disciples to "let your light shine." On the other He is saying "keep your acts of righteousness secret." Either Jesus changed His mind in the middle of His message or else He purposely confronted us with a paradox. There is a right way and a wrong way to be visible about our faith in Christ.

TRUE PIETY

If you or I were describing what it means to follow Jesus, we might have reversed the order and started with personal Bible study, prayer, church attendance, tithing, and telling people about Jesus. Instead Jesus began with ethics, the disciple's role in the secular world. The visibility Jesus called for clearly marked out our "separation from the world, our transcendence of its standards, and our extraordinariness."[1]

Now He deals with the disciple's spirituality and makes an important distinction between true piety and false piety. Ironically, being "visible" in the right way is not easy. When it comes to giving, praying, and fasting Jesus called for a secret spirituality, an unconscious holiness. True piety means relating to our heavenly Father personally without playing to an admiring audience.

This is hard in a culture given to appearances and image, publicity and self-promotion. People seem preoccupied with giving the right impression and receiving the right affirmation. If the practice of visible righteousness is absent, the vacuum will be filled by religious externals and performance. We have a natural tendency to role-play at religion when the authenticity of faith and practice has been lost or never experienced in the first place.

False piety is the kind of self-serving performance trap that turns religion into a ball and chain rather than an easy yoke. While Jesus illustrated His concern with giving, praying, and fasting, His spiritual direction extends to preaching, singing, and parenting. The issue is not between private and public spirituality, but performance-oriented religion versus a true, personal commitment to Jesus Christ. Religion tends to impose on the Christian faith expectations that tear down rather than build up our personal communion with God.

Dietrich Bonhoeffer opposed religious Christianity, and his critique exposed the underlying godlessness of religion. Religion, he contended, became a self-justifying tool for ego-centered individualism, nothing more than an attempt for self-salvation and self-expression. It was a way of meriting God's favor and impressing people with one's piety. This amounted to using God to satisfy selfish needs, placate insecurities, and domesticate the living God. Georg Huntemann writes:

> A church that allows itself to be caught up in these practices of religious pietism must face Bonhoeffer's bitter criticism: "An escapist church can be certain that it will immediately win over all the weaklings, all those who are only too glad to be lied to and deceived, all the starry-eyed dreamers, all the unborn sons of the earth." But this religious Christianity, in Bonhoeffer's opinion, opposes the saving will of Christ: "Christ does not want this weakness. Rather, he makes men and women strong. He does not lead people to fantasy worlds of religious refuge. He gives believers back to the world as its true offspring. Do not be escapist, but be strong." Thus, according to Bonhoeffer, Christian life should consist not in flight from reality, but in preservation and perseverance within reality.[2]

Bonhoeffer's hope was to replace a world-escaping, self-focused, cliché religiosity with a faith that took seriously the challenge of "religionless Christianity." Unfortunately, many have misunderstood Bonhoeffer's critique, confusing religionlessness with secularization. Bonhoeffer never meant to undermine the value of prayer or worship. On the contrary, he prayed and wrote hymns right up until his death. What he resented was artificially induced emotionalism; a "feeling like Christmas," a stylized fervor in prayer, success story power-evangelism. These were the "gods of illusion [which] must be broken and their altars burned" because they robbed the disciple of Jesus from serving the incarnate One in the real world.[3]

The Word of God reveals humankind's long history of critiquing religious acts and illustrating false piety. Aaron's vain attempt to meet the people's felt needs by building a golden calf and celebrating a "festival to the Lord" gave the people a religious experience but denied them a worship experience. The prophets offered their own version of "religionless" spirituality by reminding the people of God of the dangers of religious performance. One of God's spokesmen, Amos, declared,

> "I hate, I despise your religious feasts; I cannot stand your assemblies. Even though you bring me burnt offerings and grain offerings, I will not accept them. Though you bring choice fellowship offerings, I will have no regard for them. Away with the noise of your songs! I will not listen to the music of your harps. But let justice roll on like a river, righteousness like a never-failing stream!" (Amos 5:21-24)

Religious externals are no substitute for a person "to act justly and to love mercy and to walk humbly with your God" (Micah 6:8). Impressive church services and plenty of high-energy ministry programs may do little for drawing near to God and serving Jesus. The hallmark of true spirituality is truth from the inside out, a lesson King David learned painfully:

> Going through the motions doesn't please you, a flawless performance is nothing to you. I learned God-worship when my pride was shattered. Heart-shattered lives ready for love don't for a moment escape God's notice (Psalm 51:16-17).[4]

The critique of religion set forth by Jesus in Matthew 6 needs no commentary. The straightforward message is clearly understandable without elaborate exegesis. But that doesn't mean we understand it. Veteran disciples as well as rookies need to heed the warning, "Be especially careful when you are trying to be good so that you don't make a performance out of it. It might be good theater, but the God who made you won't be applauding" (Matthew 6:1).[5]

We fall out of spiritual shape easily. We lose our focus on God and play to the audience, hoping to win the admiration of our friends. Before we know it, what other people think of us is more important that what God thinks of us. Immediate positive human feedback takes precedence over nurturing a simple, honest relationship with God.

The message Jesus gave was as simple as "Yes" and "No": "Yes" to communion with God and "No" to performance; "Yes" to adoration and "No" to applause; "Yes" to God-worship and "No" to self-expression. Hypocrisy depends upon having an audience. Discipleship depends upon God. The spiritual disciplines are not optional for the believer. Three times Jesus says, "When you give to the needy. . . . When you pray. . . . When you fast."

The question is not whether we give, pray, or fast, but *how* we practice these disciplines. Performing these "acts of righteousness" as a way of ingratiating ourselves to others, winning their admiration, and feeding our religious pride, robs the disciplines of their singular purpose. Giving enables us to feel the compassionate heart of God; it was not meant to draw attention to our generosity. Prayer moves us into intimate, personal communion with God; it was not intended to showcase our piety. Fasting as an appetite-denying discipline helps us better concentrate on God; it was not designed to improve our rank among the pious.

Christians face the temptation of using religious practices to prove that they are respectable members in good standing. This badge of piety helps religious people to get by in life. It reminds me of the physician who was in the habit of speeding. He avoided getting a ticket by keeping a stethoscope handy in the front seat of his car. If the police tried to pull him over, he would grab his stethoscope and hold it up for the officer to see. He gave the impression that he was on the way to an emergency. This worked repeatedly until one day an officer persisted in signaling him to pull over. He looked over to find the officer holding up his gun. Giving a good impression religiously works in much the same way. Pious acts are used to convince others and sometimes even ourselves that we deserve special treatment.

External acts of righteousness may be more damaging to our spiritual health and more misleading to others than if we did nothing at all. Surely, it is precisely this hypocrisy, this play-acting, that the world is so quick to judge. Jesus makes absolutely no case for religious pragmatism. Good donors, who are not devoted disciples, do not interest Jesus. He doesn't care about Mr. Heavy-Hitter or Mr. Deep-Pockets. There are many reasons for giving that have nothing to do with helping the needy and pleasing God. People can give to relieve a guilty conscience or gain the respect of others or make themselves feel good about themselves. Fund-raisers appeal subtly to these selfish motives, but Jesus does not. He pays more attention to the heart of the widow who gives sacrificially than the big givers who get all of the attention. The Kingdom of God is built on the widow's mite. It is the difference between those who are moved by the compassion and the concern of God to give, and those who are moved by human pressure and pride to give.

God does not hear the prayer warriors, "full of formulas and programs and advice, peddling techniques for getting what you want from God."[6] God has an ear for those who pray simply—people who pray out their praise and pain in communion with God. They shift from pious self-consciousness to open-hearted prayer. In all the answering and asking, the blessing and lamenting, prayer tests our spiritual integrity. How can we ask for forgiveness if we refuse to forgive others? How can we pray, "Your will be done on earth as it is in heaven" and refuse to obey God's will? Prayer establishes a connection between what God does and what we do. Religious God-talk, designed to impress others, denies that dialogue and disconnects the relationship with God.

Untutored, we tend to think that prayer is what good people do when they are doing their best. It is not.

Inexperienced, we suppose that there must be an "insider" language that must be acquired before God takes us seriously in our prayer. There is not. Prayer is elemental, not advanced, language. It is the means by which our language becomes honest, true, and personal in response to God. It is the means by which we get everything in our lives out in the open before God.[7]

Fasting is not in vogue in today's Protestant church, but making a production out of serving the Lord certainly is. Many religious workers are addicted to leaving the impression that their busy schedules prove their spirituality. A full Day-Timer is proof of their value to Christian ministry. Breakfast and lunch meetings, afternoon appointments, four to five nights out a week all add up to significance. Judging from the photo covers of celebrity-saints, current religious culture has reversed the dress code and revolutionized the saintly image. Religion has lost the haggard look, opting for something more sexy and successful. The issue, however, is still appearance versus reality, and God is never fooled.

Fasting is important for the followers of Jesus as a discipline affirming our dependence upon God. Through fasting we can identify with the hungry and needy. We can check our propensity for self-indulgent appetites and remind ourselves that the body was made for God. Fasting can reinforce repentance and confession and focus our attention on God. Fasting remains a relevant spiritual discipline as long as its motives are pure. It is a spiritual discipline that works below the surface strengthening our personal relationship with God. Turn it into an occasion for personal publicity and religious merit and it becomes a spiritual evil.

The difference between religious performance and authentic acts of devotion to God is like the difference between schooling and education. It is all too easy to go through the motions, do relatively well on tests, get passing grades, and yet learn almost nothing in the process. It's scary to read of such a high percentage of high school graduates who don't know how to read. An even scarier thought is that a person could attend church regularly, give an offering weekly, and ten years from now say that he or she never heard the gospel through Doug Webster's preaching. Imagine giving, praying, and working in the church for years and never experiencing the grace of the Lord Jesus Christ. Such people are carrying around the burden of religious duty, paying their religious dues, taking pride in religious works and never really knowing the heavenly Father.

THE "SECRET" OF PUBLIC PRAYER

Our first reaction to Jesus' teaching may be to insist that the spiritual disciplines are completely private. A simplistic reading of Jesus' critique eliminates corporate worship and public prayer. But this is not what Jesus had in mind. It was not His purpose to privatize spirituality but to authenticate true spirituality. He wanted to take the performance and production out of corporate worship and purify the motives behind personal and corporate spirituality. God-focused worship causes the Body of Christ to pay attention to God as the primary audience.

Churches need to be careful not to slip into a performance mode. Today's emphasis on felt needs and entertainment increases the possibility that religious leaders will fall into the performance trap. That is one reason why we must discipline ourselves to direct our attention to God, not as an excuse for boring religious services, but as an inspiration for authentic worship. I am confident that as the people of God pray and fast and earnestly seek God's will in their worship, they will know the difference between religious performance and spiritual power, theatrical production and theological perception, excellence in form and holiness in practice.

MODELING HIDDEN RIGHTEOUSNESS

The most solid witness to authentic spirituality comes quietly and unobtrusively. When I read Jesus' spiritual direction on giving, I think of an elderly woman in Toronto, Lillian Softley, who quietly gave to meet the needs of others. Her own simple living actually gave the impression she had little to give, but it was that simple living that enabled her to give to others.

When I was a doctoral student I was a recipient of one of Lillian's gifts. She had heard that we were trying to make a down payment on a townhouse. She approached me as humbly and as graciously as if she were asking for help from me, rather than offering to give me help. With Lillian's no interest loan we were able to pay the down payment, but the impact of her spirit went way beyond her financial help. She gave me the distinct impression that the gift was between herself and God.

Jesus' teaching on prayer reminds me of Mrs. Van Dyck, a former missionary to China, whom I met when she was bedridden in a nursing home. I was sixteen. I went to minister to her, to encourage an elderly Christian woman. It didn't take me long to figure out who was ministering to whom. Her body was extremely weak, but her spirit was very strong. Mrs. Van Dyck was a person of prayer. I went to her thinking how miserable it must be to be so weak that you could not get out of bed. But I always left impressed with the power of God. Prayer seemed to transform her 12' by 12' room into a vast mission field. She was not defined by the limitations of her body but by the vitality and power of her praying imagination. She meant nothing impressive by this and expected no attention.

When I read what Jesus says on fasting I think of a student from Guyana named Ram Kalap. Following our regular weekly class on Tuesdays, I asked him to lunch several times. He declined politely. One day I pressed him for a reason and he reluctantly told me that Tuesday was the day he fasted. Ram, like many of the foreign students at the Bible college, practiced the spiritual disciplines of prayer and fasting without drawing attention to himself. It was part of his "secret" relationship with the Lord. He looked for a reward that human approval and applause could not give him.

THE PAYOFF

Make no mistake, the practice of hidden righteousness is evident in the believer's quiet dependence upon God and unflaunted spirituality. The intimacy and significance of this personal communion with God may be reward enough. Three times Jesus stressed that our acts of righteousness are to be done in secret. Three times he affirmed, "Then your Father, who sees what is done in secret, will reward you."

Besides the eternal rewards promised by God for faithfulness, there are immediate benefits. One of those benefits is the assurance of genuine fulfillment. The reward for our effort is the fruit of our labor. The needs of the needy are met. Prayer is honest communion with God. Fasting affirms our dependence upon God. Certainly, part of the reward for hidden righteousness is experienced in the consummation of our effort and in our deepening relationship with God.

C. S. Lewis, in his essay *The Weight of Glory*, writes, "There are different kinds of rewards. There is the reward which has no natural connection with the things you do to earn it and is quite foreign to the desires that ought to accompany these things."[8] My father tells the story of the time he participated in a hot dog eating contest. He won the contest, but the prize, which had not been announced beforehand, turned out to be less than appealing. It was a huge hot fudge sundae, which he was unable to eat.

If a person gives or prays or fasts for public acclaim, it's like a person marrying for money instead of love. "But marriage is the proper reward for a real lover," observes Lewis. "The proper rewards are not simply tacked on to the activity for which they are given, but are the activity itself in consummation."[9] The proper reward for good parenting is not the envy of your neighbors but a good relationship with your daughter or son.

Another benefit to secret righteousness is the affirmation it gives to our personal relationship with God. "For a human being to be truly human, it is very important that he or she has a sense of the secret of the self. Jesus honors this inner mystery about what it means to be fully human."[10] Spirituality from the inside out has the important effect of revealing to ourselves the importance of our relationship to our heavenly Father. Who we are in private was meant to be consistent with who we are in public. Corporate worship was designed to grow out of personal devotion.

Abraham learned the incredible lesson of what it feels like to value his relationship with God above everything else, even the life of his son. Job experienced a persevering passion for God even though there was no worldly, human reason for remaining faithful to God. It is in this personal state of aloneness with God, when all other considerations are abandoned, that our true relationship with God is revealed to us.

Taking up the easy yoke liberates us from pretense and performance. Hidden righteousness turns religion into relationship and ritual into worship. We no longer feel strange and foreign in the presence of God. We are there, not out of duty or for the approval of others, but out of personal love for God in Christ. Publicity and promotion only serve to distract from the real work at hand: "to know Christ and the power of his resurrection and the fellowship of sharing in his sufferings, becoming like him in his death" (Philippians 3:10). When it comes to rest for the soul, it's what's below the surface that counts.

Let me conclude by pointing out that at each stage in the Sermon on the Mount the cost of discipleship is measured against the cost of nondiscipleship. The question is asked, Is it easier to be yoked to Jesus or to be left alone to do our own thing? We have reasoned that without a vital connection to Jesus, living the Christian life is not only difficult, it is impossible.

Sadly, the world sees more religious performance than it does beatitude-based behavior. Without the easy yoke, believers have a natural tendency to reverse the spiritual order of things, putting on public display what was meant to be personal and refusing to demonstrate practically what was meant to be public. For our own good Jesus takes us below the surface and examines the motives and practices of true spirituality. To be yoked to Christ is a blessing, not a burden. It makes the difference between liberation and bondage, especially in the spiritual disciplines of prayer, giving, and fasting.

"*Be* especially careful when you are trying to be good so that you don't make a performance out of it. It might be good theater, but the God who made you won't be applauding.

"When you do something for someone else, don't call attention to yourself. You've seen them in action, I'm sure—'playactors' I call them—treating prayer meeting and street corner alike as a stage, acting compassionate as long as someone is watching, playing to the crowds. They get applause, true, but that's all they get. When you help someone out, don't think about how it looks. Just do it—quietly and unobtrusively. That is the way your God, who conceived you in love, working behind the scenes, helps you out.

"And when you come before God, don't turn that into a theatrical production either. All these people making a regular show out of their prayers, hoping for stardom! Do you think God sits in a box seat?

"Here's what I want you to do: Find a quiet, secluded place so you won't be tempted to role-play before God. Just be there as simply and honestly as you can manage. The focus will shift from you to God, and you will begin to sense his grace.

"When you practice some appetite-denying discipline to better concentrate on God, don't make a production out of it. It might turn you into a small-time celebrity but it won't make you a saint. If you 'go into training' inwardly, act normal outwardly. Shampoo and comb your hair, brush your teeth, wash your face. God doesn't require attention-getting devices. He won't overlook what you are doing; he'll reward you well."

MATTHEW 6:1-6,16-18; *THE MESSAGE*

"*Do* not store up for yourselves treasures on earth, where moth and rust destroy, and where thieves break in and steal. But store up for yourselves treasures in heaven, where moth and rust do not destroy, and where thieves do not break in and steal. For where your treasure is, there your heart will be also.

"The eye is the lamp of the body. If your eyes are good, your whole body will be full of light. But if your eyes are bad, your whole body will be full of darkness. If then the light within you is darkness, how great is that darkness!

"No one can serve two masters. Either he will hate the one and love the other, or he will be devoted to the one and despise the other. You cannot serve both God and Money."

MATTHEW 6:19-24

CHAPTER ELEVEN

Values, Vision, and Loyalties

Jesus is in the business of redefining *easy.*

He gives us back the life we have lost in the living. He brings order out of chaos, clarity out of clutter. Instead of information, He offers wisdom. Instead of communication, He encourages communion. Instead of the self-styled, fashionable personality, He mentors God-centered, God-honoring character. He establishes a rhythm between work and worship, prayer and play, rest and restlessness. Jesus calls us to new priorities, perspectives, and preferences. He offers us "a practical commentary on living according to the Lord's prayer."[1]

Real estate ads offer an interesting perspective on easy living: custom-built, luxury homes, beautifully situated on spacious lots. The ads describe plush landscaping, a great view, plenty of privacy, tennis courts, pools, convenient shopping, excellent schools, golf courses . . . who could ask for anything more? Everything anybody could want for easy living, but not necessarily everything needed for living well. Interestingly enough, these real estate ads don't picture people. We see beautiful family rooms without families, immaculate yards without the kids playing catch, and gorgeous living rooms that have never been lived in.

At the corner of Bloor and Avenue Roads in downtown

Toronto there was a sign just before the Church of the Redeemer that read "Discover the Art of Living." As one walked west on Bloor, it appeared to be a sign for the church. It was not. It was an advertisement for a new luxury condominium being built next door. The sign captured the wisdom of the age: The art of living is knowing where to live—in a luxury "condo"—not how to live.

Clearly, what the world means by easy living is not what Jesus meant by the easy yoke. His description of visible righteousness and hidden righteousness is practical but not pragmatic, understandable but not immediately accessible, and convicting yet inconvenient. The strategy of Jesus for living is not packaged for easy consumption. Today's laid-back, easygoing, connect-the-dots, paint-by-number Christianity, on sale everywhere, is not found in the Sermon on the Mount.

After we come to Christ, there is no such thing as business as usual. If we were ever tempted to think that we could follow Jesus and keep the status quo, this text pronounces a decisive "No." The disciple is called to make a choice. "Do not store up for yourselves treasures on earth. . . . But store up for yourselves treasures in heaven, where moth and rust do not destroy, and where thieves do not break in and steal" (Matthew 6:19).

Jesus used three metaphors to capture the driving force behind our ambition, vision, and devotion. First, What are we living for? "For where your treasure is, there your heart will be also" (verse 21). Second, What is the focus of our attention? "If your eyes are good, your whole body will be full of light" (verse 22). And third, Whom are we serving? "No one can serve two masters" (verse 24). Jesus deals with our life-controlling priorities, perspectives, and preferences.

WHAT ARE YOUR AMBITIONS?

Our attitude toward money is especially helpful in understanding how secure we are under the easy yoke. If you were to lose $100,000 of your hard-earned money, how would it change your life? Several years ago scores of investors were faced with just that challenge. They had invested with a highly respected and trusted Christian who traded in stock options. He promised an annual 20 percent return on their investment. It was almost too good to be true. Some shifted all their investments and retirement programs to his company, and for several years everything went along fine. Christian organizations benefited from the broker's philanthropy and many people received unusually high yields.

But the company was not doing as well as everyone thought, and the 20 percent return was funded through new investments and roll-over profits. In fact, the company was losing money. Out of desperation the broker committed 90 percent of the company's funds to United Airlines Stock Options, even though he had promised investors he would never put more than 10 percent of the investment portfolio into any one deal. Two days later the Gulf War broke out and United Airlines' stocks fell significantly, wiping out millions in assets. The financial and emotional impact for many was great; for some it was devastating. Everyone involved was upset, some embittered. For the church where many of the investors were members, it was a wake-up call. The words of Jesus, "For where your treasure is, there your heart will be also," began to take on new meaning.

Some who lost money put the entire onus on the broker, charging that he had falsified the books and lied to investors. Others felt the sting of their own foolishness, embarrassed over the greed that led them to invest so much in a speculative venture.

When I visited the broker in prison, I met a broken man who had fallen from the pedestal into the pit. We talked about what success had done to his marriage. When he was everybody's hero he was consumed with a passion for making money. He was married to his business. While he was impressing Christian organizations with his generosity, he was starving his soul. Nobody challenged his priorities then; everybody wanted him to succeed.

Sitting in prison, he admitted his failure and expressed his remorse. Yet he still wonders how much worse he was than the people who flirted with greed and benefited for so long from his success. Prison has given him time with God, the time he did not have for so long when he was storing up treasures on earth. He has rediscovered the Word of God. He is leading some Bible studies and taking a Bible correspondence program. "God knew I needed prison," he said. "It may be the best thing that ever happened to me. I see what is important now."

Jesus did not intend the metaphor of the two treasures to eliminate financial investment and savings accounts. In fact, if the New York Stock Exchange on Wall Street were looking for a good verse to put over its front entrance, this would be a great one. "For where your treasure is, there your heart will be also." Precious commodities in Jesus' day, such as expensive garments, fine foods, and precious metals, were vulnerable to decay and thieves.

In time, every material object becomes like a used car or an obsolete computer. What's sold at Nordstrom ends up at Goodwill. Multimillion dollar properties go up in smoke or slide down the hill. The point of the contrast between Heaven and earth focuses on the object of our security. "For where your treasure is, there your heart will be also." "The heart represents the 'control center' and stands for the ultimate direction of one's innermost desires."[2]

WHAT IS THE FOCUS OF YOUR ATTENTION?

Jesus adds to the point already made when he says, "The eye is the lamp of the body." As Eugene H. Peterson said, "If you open your eyes wide in wonder and belief, your body fills up with light. If you live squinty-eyed in greed and distrust, your body is a dank cellar."[3] If the treasure is a metaphor for ambition, the eye is a metaphor for vision. With the eyes of faith, we can discern light and darkness, good and evil. Like a trained artist, we can see what is really there. We can see the real world.

We need a whole new way of seeing life that integrates the

totality of life from the perspective of Kingdom values. Recently, when I had my vision tested, they checked for all sorts of problems, including glaucoma, depth perception, tunnel vision, and color blindness. Most of the tests involved focusing straight ahead. Eyes that are in perfect health are able to see clearly and in color. They can see close up and at a distance. They can see the center as well as the periphery. Likewise, Kingdom vision can see comprehensively and apply God's truth to the full range of human issues.

Jesus is calling us to cultivate an eye for truth. Open your eyes wide so you can see how it really is. Don't get trapped by the evil eye of greed and envy. Look at everything in the light of Christ.

WHO IS YOUR MASTER?

Ultimately it comes down to this: "No one can serve two masters. Either he will hate the one and love the other, or he will be devoted to the one and despise the other." Jesus exposes a conflict of interest bigger than any political scandal or insider trading-scheme. We cannot have it both ways. Jesus calls for total allegiance, single-minded devotion. Middle-of-the-road Christianity is not an option. Praying the prayer Jesus taught His disciples leads us to choose a standard of living.

Do we really mean it when we pray, "Your kingdom come, your will be done on earth as it is in heaven"? For feel-good Christians on the make, this passage says, "Time out!" Time for a reality check. Jesus is not our chaplain, He's our master. He hasn't come to bless our business, He has come to take it over. Jesus is not offering an improvement plan. He calls for total commitment and absolute allegiance. He's not remodeling and redecorating the existing structure. He is starting over with a new blueprint, new building materials on a whole new site.

We should feel like the trespasser who accidentally found a hidden treasure in an otherwise worthless field. He immediately sold everything he had to purchase the field. We are like the jewel merchant who discovered a flawless pearl and liquidated all his assets to buy it. Jesus offers a high-stakes, all-or-nothing investment strategy. Jesus dispels the both/and option and calls for an either/or decision.

LIMITATION CAN BE LIBERATION

It was Sören Kierkegaard, the Danish philosopher, who said the principle of limitation is the only saving principle in the world. The more you limit yourself, the more creative and inventive you will be. Professionals choose an area of expertise and then concentrate their attention. Physicians, musicians, CPA's, teachers, and contractors all specialize. They do this out of necessity. Making these career-defining decisions is not easy, but it is essential. For the decision-maker, the choice is crucial. It cannot be put off indefinitely without loss of opportunity. The decision is not arbitrary; the pros and cons are considered thoroughly because the consequences are life-changing.

Marriage illustrates this principle of limitation as well. A man and a woman pledge themselves to one another—the language of their vows is grandly inclusive of all they are and will be. This comprehensive commitment is also a timeless commitment: "As long as our lives shall last" is the bottom line of a costly vow. Self-fulfillment through self-limitation is a blessing, not a curse. Intimacy and security are not possible apart from an enduring commitment.

Today's cultural ethos of keeping our options open affects the follower of Jesus in this area as well. Our incapacity to commit ourselves to anyone or anything lest we feel trapped or locked in makes single-minded devotion to Christ more difficult. We find it easier to devote ourselves to short-term interests and trivial pursuits. We are devoted to consumer products, sports teams, and recreational pursuits. We are more defined by our leisure activities than we are by our spiritual disciplines. The Peter Pan syndrome is what psychologists call the reluctance or incapacity of adults to grow up and make adult commitments. We want to be free to do our own thing when we want to do it. We are afraid we might miss something. A new spouse, a new career, a new adventure, a new car; we are always looking for something more out of living. But more is never better, it's just different.

Many people may be surprised to learn that Jesus does have a "Go for the Gold!" philosophy of life. As Dietrich Bonhoeffer wrote, "Jesus knows that the human heart hankers after a treasure, and so it is his will that we should have one. But this treasure is to be sought in heaven, not on earth. Earthly treasures soon fade, but a treasure in heaven lasts forever. . . . Jesus does not deprive the human heart of its instinctive needs—treasure, glory, and praise. But he gives it higher objects—the glory of God (John 5:44), the glorying in the cross (Galatians 6:14), and treasure in heaven."[4]

The problem is that we have a tendency to scale down our expectations. In our effort to get more, we come up with less. "Our Lord finds our desires not too strong, but too weak," writes C. S. Lewis. "We are half-hearted creatures, fooling about with drink and sex and ambition when infinite joy is offered us, like an ignorant child who wants to go on making mud pies in a slum because he cannot imagine what is meant by the offer of a holiday at the sea. We are far too easily pleased."[5]

From the beginning to end of his career, a friend of mine, Dan Lam, was successful, but that is not what he will be remembered for. He came to Christ as a boy in his native Hong Kong. His father died when he was young and he was raised by his mother, whose strength and devotion marked Dan's life. He grew up poor, determined to work hard and be a success. Years later, Dan attended a retreat, hosted by John Stott, pastor of All Soul's Church in London. Dan was headquartered in London, working on construction projects on three continents, supervising fifteen hundred employees. On the retreat he became convicted about Kingdom values and the believer's simple lifestyle. He began to realize that the gospel not only converts the soul but transforms the life. He remained an active businessman, but his focus became different. He wanted to use his time, energy, and resources to further the Kingdom of Christ. Business success became the mere means to that end. Money lost its priority.

I first met Dan about three years ago. His reputation preceded our first encounter. Dan was broad-shouldered, tall, quick-witted and eager. The pastoral staff affectionately called Dan "the Asian invasion." I was told he was a visionary with a passion for Christ. He was committed to proclaiming the gospel among the unreached. He was a confident, single-minded individual with a mission. The Holy Spirit sanctified his entrepreneurial spirit, making him a gentle crusader, a tentmaker missionary. He could put a peasant farmer in Burma at ease and be every bit the equal to a high roller in Hong Kong.

Because of Christ's work through Dan, there are hundreds of Vietnamese pastors preaching the gospel. Scores of Cambodian believers are studying the Bible. Mongolians are being taught the fundamentals of Christian theology, and Russians in Siberia are growing in their faith.

We first met, by appointment, in my office. He came in, paced the floor for a moment or two, then emptied his pockets of his wallet, keys, and pen, as was his custom. He took off his watch and glasses and sat down. His charming, can-do grin was part of his protocol, his grace-filled greeting. But he always got down to business quickly. He never wasted time.

"I want you to disciple me," he said. "Can you do it?"

Knowing what I knew about Dan, I said, "I think it would be better the other way around."

"No, can you disciple me?"

"Okay, how about we disciple one another?" I proposed.

"No, I don't have time for you. Can you disciple me? I need somebody to pray for me and discuss God's work. I need someone to hold me accountable."

That started a friendship, a partnership in the gospel, that took me to Mongolia twice. Dan was so much a servant of God that he became my boss. God was moving and working so powerfully within Dan and blessing his ministry that I decided early on I had little choice but to pay attention.

"Doug, I need a course outline and curriculum for the first year of Bible school in Mongolia by next week." If I hesitated, he piled on all the reasons why I should do this and how much easier it was for me to do it than it was for him. Dan was decisive. He despised the bureaucracy and lethargy of many mission organizations. Dan had a real bottom line theology. He kept his eyes focused on Jesus. He was determined not to get bogged down in petty problems and manmade obstacles. He embodied for me what it means to seek first Christ's Kingdom and His righteousness.

Dan was restless for the sake of the Kingdom; networking, facilitating, empowering a whole range of Christians, from indigenous pastors in Southeast Asia, to new believers in Mongolia, to North American seminary professors. Other people talk about being global or world Christians; Dan embodied it. For years he has been a literal ambassador for Christ, engaging in global shuttle diplomacy for the Kingdom of Christ.

On March 22, 1994, Aeroflot Flight 593, carrying Dan on a flight from Moscow to Hong Kong, crashed in Russia. All seventy-five on board were killed. The believing community mourned the loss of a true ambassador for Christ. I don't know if Daniel Lam was conscious of living on the edge for Christ, but I do know he was truly willing to lose his life for the sake of the gospel. Dan shared the passion of Jesus. Every day was a choice between ambitions, visions, and masters—and every day Jesus won.

Ironically, the broker I visited in jail, whose life was in shambles because of misplaced values, vision, and loyalties, went to the same church Dan went to. They were friends, brothers in Christ, but only one of them knew the experience of the easy yoke and the light burden. On this side of eternity it is never too late to make the choice for Christ and His Kingdom. This either/or decision not only counts for eternity, but it lightens the burden and gives rest for the soul. "Our Father in heaven, hallowed be your name. Your kingdom come, your will be done on earth as it is in heaven. Give us this day our daily bread." To pray that prayer changes the way we live.

"*D*on't hoard treasure down here where it gets eaten by moths and corroded by rust or—worse! stolen by burglars. Stockpile treasure in heaven, where it's safe from moth and rust and burglars. It's obvious, isn't it? The place where your treasure is, is the place you will most want to be, and end up being.

"Your eyes are windows into your body. If you open your eyes wide in wonder and belief, your body fills up with light. If you live squinty-eyed in greed and distrust, your body is a dank cellar. If you pull the blinds on your windows, what a dark life you will have!

"You can't worship two gods at once. Loving one god, you'll end up hating the other. Adoration of one feeds contempt for the other. You can't worship God and Money both."

MATTHEW 6:19-24, *THE MESSAGE*

"*Therefore I tell you, do not worry about your life, what you will eat or drink; or about your body, what you will wear. Is not life more important than food, and the body more important than clothes? Look at the birds of the air; they do not sow or reap or store away in barns, and yet your heavenly Father feeds them. Are you not much more valuable than they? Who of you by worrying can add a single hour to his life?

"And why do you worry about clothes? See how the lilies of the field grow. They do not labor or spin. Yet I tell you that not even Solomon in all his splendor was dressed like one of these. If that is how God clothes the grass of the field, which is here today and tomorrow is thrown into the fire, will he not much more clothe you, O you of little faith? So do not worry, saying, 'What shall we eat?' or 'What shall we drink?' or 'What shall we wear?' For the pagans run after all these things, and your heavenly Father knows that you need them. But seek first his kingdom and his righteousness, and all these things will be given to you as well. Therefore do not worry about tomorrow, for tomorrow will worry about itself. Each day has enough trouble of its own.

"Do not judge, or you too will be judged. For in the same way you judge others, you will be judged, and with the measure you use, it will be measured to you.

"Why do you look at the speck of sawdust in your brother's eye and pay no attention to the plank in your own eye? How can you say to your brother, 'Let me take the speck out of your eye,' when all the time there is a plank in your own eye? You hypocrite, first take the plank out of your own eye, and then you will see clearly to remove the speck from your brother's eye.

"Do not give dogs what is sacred; do not throw your pearls to pigs. If you do, they may trample them under their feet, and then turn and tear you to pieces.

"Ask and it will be given to you; seek and you will find; knock and the door will be opened to you. For everyone who asks receives; he who seeks finds; and to him who knocks, the door will be opened.

"Which of you, if his son asks for bread, will give him a stone? Or if he asks for a fish, will give him a snake? If you, then, though you are evil, know how to give good gifts to your children, how much more will your Father in heaven give good gifts to those who ask him! So in everything, do to others what you would have them do to you, for this sums up the Law and the Prophets."

MATTHEW 6:25–7:12

CHAPTER TWELVE

Lighten Up

Beatitude believers were not called to burn out. Salt and light saints were not meant to feel strung out. There is a difference between being persecuted for righteousness' sake and being frustrated by habits, false expectations, and pious pressures that Jesus never intended the disciple to assume.

One happy task of a spiritual director or a pastor is to disabuse people of unholy burdens. It is easier, of course, to learn how to do it right the first time. If we pay attention to what Jesus has to say, we may avoid some unnecessary struggles and disappointments. It would be nice if Winston Churchill's wry comment on Americans was not true of Christians: "You can always count on Americans to do the right thing after they have exhausted all other possibilities."

Living under the easy yoke calls for distinguishing between true and false expectations. It calls for discerning the difference between obedience and self-imposed obligations; between devotion to God and religious duty. Wisdom identifies the path of discipleship and exposes religious peer pressure. There is nothing that will kill the spirit of the disciple faster than a critical spirit. Nothing will dampen the joy of the Lord more than one-upmanship righteousness. Make evangelism an imposed duty, a technique to be performed, a message to be forced on others, and the gospel of grace becomes a burden.

Some well-intentioned believers react to religious rigidity and compulsion by offering a casual, feel-good, user-friendly Christianity. Veterans of church quarrels and fights, they want a happier version of Christianity. Tired of doctrinal debates, personality conflicts, and hassles over social issues, they want their Christianity positive and upbeat. Instead of a pulpit-pounding harangue, they want an inspiring, uplifting sermon. In their attempt to avoid judgmentalism and a negative spirit, they opt for a people-pleasing gospel, comprised of seriously unserious sermons, entertaining worship, and low commitment converts. Much of American Christianity is a reaction to self-righteous legalism, manipulative evangelism, and pious spiritualizing.

However, the popular solution does not solve the practical problem. It only makes it worse. Judgmentalism is not solved by the absence of spiritual accountability, nor is guilt-induced, manipulative evangelism corrected by felt-need focused, market-driven evangelism. Replacing legalism with license and substituting self-help for being Spirit-led does not encourage discipleship.

The easy yoke is an alternative to both a critical spirit and spiritual complacency. It offers spiritual direction that resists religious peer pressure on the one hand and private autonomy on the other. The strategy of Jesus removes the burden of overly zealous piety and demonstrates the difference between religious fanaticism and true-hearted spiritual passion. "The great task of the disciple is to recognize the limits of their commission," wrote Bonhoeffer.[1] If we fail to learn these limits we fall susceptible to frustrations and pressures foreign to the life Jesus intended for us to live. The Apostle Paul reminds us, "For we are God's workmanship created in Christ Jesus to do good works, which God prepared in advance for us to do."

CALL OR OBSESSION?

I have a friend who recently discovered he was causing his body more harm than good from too much exercise. Convinced that more and more of a good thing could only be better, he had pushed his body to perform at an ever-increasing level of intensity. Studies have shown, however, that exercising at a maximum heart rate for more than 75 percent of a workout wears the body down. Knowing that, he bought a heart monitor to pace himself. He is now careful to run at his peak heart rate for only 20 percent of his workout. The results have been noticeable. He has more energy, sleeps better, and feels healthier. What is true physically is also true spiritually.

In Matthew 6:25–7:12 Jesus identifies four subtle forms of spiritual distortion: excessive worry, judgmental accountability, forced evangelism, and protracted prayer. Contrary to popular opinion, these activities do not build up the Body of Christ, they wear it out. Many Christians labor under a false expectation of what is required of them. They succumb to internal and external religious pressure that needlessly increases the burden of the Christian life. They are subtle because they are cloaked in righteousness. They are dangerous, because when yielded to, they ruin our spiritual life. If we are serious about following Jesus we will want to watch out for these false expectations and pressures.

EXCESSIVE WORRY

For many, worry is to living what air is to breathing. But Jesus says this is not the way it is with His disciples. "I tell you, do not worry about your life, what you will eat or drink; or about your body, what you will wear." Bible-believing Christians are in danger of missing today's opportunities for fear of tomorrow's problems. Some believers are convinced that the most spiritual thing to do is worry over the future: the coming economic collapse, the collapse of the nuclear family, the educational crisis, the fear of getting cancer, the growing violence in our streets. Peruse the shelves in a Christian bookstore and you may wonder if today's Christian is not driven more by fear than faith.

"The present situation," says Os Guinness, "is reminiscent

of the 1920's quip about a fundamentalist being someone who 'talks of standing on the rock of ages, but acts as if he were clinging to the last piece of driftwood.'"[2] We pray, "Our Father in heaven . . . for thine is the Kingdom and the Power and the Glory forever," but we worry as if God were not sovereign and the world was going to hell in a hand basket. We are more like Chicken Little, who ran around shouting, "The sky is falling! The sky is falling!"

Christ-centered concern becomes worthless worry when we fail to exercise faith in the Lord of the universe. Concern leads us to trust in God. Worry produces anxiety. Concern develops in the disciple a deeper understanding of evil and redemption. Worry sensationalizes evil and feeds on fear. Faith produces insight and perseverance, but the end product of worry is resentment and retaliation.

It is almost as if Jesus read the minds of the disciples before the question was on their lips. What does it mean practically to serve God instead of money? Jesus makes the connection between the sovereignty of God and the family budget. What follows speaks to everything from personal contentment to church growth strategies. "Therefore I tell you, do not worry about your life, what you will eat or drink; or about your body, what you will wear" (Matthew 6:25).

Perhaps it is this confusion between what is right and what works that makes following Jesus so difficult. It is difficult to step out in faith and believe that what is right actually works. Maybe it doesn't work the way the world measures success, but it works the way God measures success. Tested over time, the easy yoke is more fulfilling than frustrating, more effective than efficient, more practical than pragmatic and more faithful than fashionable. Instead of using people up and burning them out, the easy yoke gives them strength and endurance, patience and perseverance. The easy yoke gives us back the life we lost in the living.

Jesus does not rule out responsible living. He did not say, "Take no thought." He said, "Do not worry." Nor did Jesus equate anxious thought with hard work. What He forbids is a "crippling anxiety that drives one to seek security by one's own efforts apart from the Father."[3] When we stop looking to our heavenly Father and start looking to ourselves, we are in trouble. Even the basic necessities of life were meant to become the raw material for trust in God.

We can say all we want about our heart being right with God and our devotion being to Him alone, but if we are constantly fretting about food or medicine or rent or car payments, our commitment is empty rhetoric. A refusal to worry and complain proves the integrity of our ambition to please God, our vision of God, and our devotion to God.

Jesus illustrates His point by showing off the birds and the wildflowers. Birds have plenty to eat without even raising, harvesting, and storing food. Flowers look great without ever giving a thought to their appearance. Why worry? Don't be consumed by consumable products. Don't be possessed by your possessions. Get a life. Trust in your heavenly Father. If birds and flowers make out so well, how much more will you.

Jesus might have worded this challenge differently if He were writing to Americans. "How dare you rest your self-esteem on the clothes you wear or take pride in your gourmet food. Why are you so preoccupied with appearances and adventures that money can buy? Are you any different from the people who don't even believe that I exist? Where are your priorities? What really counts in life anyway, financial security or eternal security? Stop thinking about more, more, more, getting, getting, getting. Life cannot be measured with a calculator and a W-2 form."

William Willimon tells the story of a recruiter for the "Teach America" program. She was at Duke attempting to interest prospective teachers to work in especially difficult and deprived school systems. To an auditorium full of Duke students, she said,

> "Looking at you tonight, I don't know why I'm here.
> You are privileged, the beneficiaries of the best of this

nation's educational resources. I can tell, just by looking at you, that you are all bound for Wall Street, law school, medical school. And here I stand, trying to recruit you for a salary of $15,000 a year in some of the worst school situations in America, begging you to waste your life for a bunch of ungrateful kids in the backwoods of Appalachia or the inner city of Philadelphia. I must have been crazy to come here.

"But I do have some literature up here, and I would be willing to talk to anybody who happens to be interested. But I know, just by looking at you, that all of you want to be a success, and here I am inviting you to be failures. So you can all leave now. But if by chance somebody here feels called to do the worst job any of you can imagine, then I'm here to talk to you. The meeting's over."

With that, everyone stood up and stampeded to the front, fighting over a chance to talk to this recruiter, just dying to give their lives to something more interesting than conventional American success, dying to give themselves to something bigger and more important than themselves.[4]

JUDGMENTALISM

At times I wish Jesus were more like a lawyer than a prophet. He makes bold, stark statements that can be easily misconstrued. Because He doesn't carefully nuance His admonitions or qualify His commands, His words seem more vulnerable to misrepresentation. Since He knew the human propensity to take things wrong, to lift His words out of context, why did He say so bluntly, "Do not judge, or you too will be judged"? If we isolate these words, would it be possible to conclude that Jesus is an advocate for a laissez-faire tolerance, a live and let live philosophy of life? Everything Jesus said must be understood in the larger context of what He meant.

One of the churches described in the book of Revelation is

a case in point. There may have been professing Christians in the church in Pergamum who quoted from the Sermon on the Mount to defend their unholy diversity. The early Church struggled with the tension between a gospel of grace and a life of discipleship. It was not easy to be open to all people and holding one another morally and spiritually accountable. The Apostle John's critique of the potentially fatal compromise in Pergamum was explicit: "You have people there who hold to the teaching of Balaam, who taught Balak to entice the Israelites to sin by eating food sacrificed to idols and by committing sexual immorality. Likewise you also have those who hold to the teaching of the Nicolaitans. Repent therefore! Otherwise, I will soon come to you and will fight against them with the sword of my mouth" (Revelation 2:14-16). Undoubtedly, the Pergamum congregation was made up of faithful believers in the tradition of Antipas, who was martyred for the faith, and compromising believers, who espoused the teaching of the Nicolaitans.

Scholars inform us that some early believers distinguished between the soul, which was saved by grace, and the flesh which was destined to die. Thus, what a person did in his body had no spiritual implications for the soul. This body/soul dichotomy rationalized sexual and material indulgence. Instead of integrating the whole person in a life of faithfulness, they believed they could compartmentalize existence and discount acts of evil done in the flesh. This proved to be a convenient way of avoiding the cost of discipleship and the challenge of church discipline. Tolerance and diversity were the watchword.

It would be easier, from a worldly point of view, if we could define diversity and tolerance according to the moral fashions of our day. Lately, I have heard Jesus' prohibition, "Do not judge!" quoted by Christians who do not want sinful practices to be identified as sin. "Jesus did not come to condemn the world," they say, "but to save the world. It is not our place to judge our fellow Christian. Let him who has no sin cast the first stone." This counsel sounds spiritual, but it is based on a misunderstanding of Jesus' warning. It confuses moral discernment with judgmentalism.

Whatever else Jesus meant, He did not mean we should ignore the road that leads to destruction or fail to inspect for bad fruit or be fooled by a wolf in sheep's clothing. Jesus' warning, "Do not judge," is surely consistent with His warning against false lifestyles, false teachers, and bad apples. Righteousness involves distinguishing between good and evil. Judgmentalism, on the other hand, means picking on people, jumping on their failures, criticizing their faults.

The Apostle Paul wrote to the Ephesians similar spiritual direction: "Get rid of all bitterness, rage and anger, brawling and slander, along with every form of malice. Be kind and compassionate to one another, forgiving each other, just as in Christ God forgave you." Forgiveness, however, does not become an excuse for condoning evil. Paul goes on to say, "But among you there must not be even a hint of sexual immorality, or of any kind of impurity, or of greed, because these are improper for God's holy people. . . . Have nothing to do with the fruitless deeds of darkness, but rather expose them" (4:31; 5:3,11).

Discernment and discipline are dimensions of biblical love we cannot afford to live without. "This is my prayer," wrote Paul, "that your love may abound more and more in knowledge and depth of insight, so that you may be able to discern what is best and may be pure and blameless until the day of Christ, filled with the fruit of righteousness that comes through Jesus Christ—to the glory and praise of God" (Philippians 1:9-11). Offering timely correction and meaningful discipline is not the work of a critical spirit, but of the Holy Spirit. As we all know, it is fundamental to good parenting and basic to developing the household of faith.

Distinguishing between discernment and judgmentalism is critical. One is absolutely essential to the Church, and the other is most detrimental. Instead of wisely identifying sin, offering healthy moral accountability, and discerning spiritual direction, church members can excel in backbiting, gossip, and slander.

Churches that carp and complain against one another invariably turn a blind eye to blatant violations of God's will. Their moral insensitivity is matched by their selfish preferences and personal biases. Many of the internal problems churches suffer have nothing to do with taking a moral stand and exercising church discipline. Rather, they have to do with bruised egos, competitive musical tastes, personality conflicts, and disagreements over money. Jesus warns against our readiness to spot the speck in our neighbor's eye, while remaining blind to the beam in our own eye. Don't be so quick to take offense, Jesus insists. For those who pray, "Forgive us our debts as we forgive our debtors," our first order of business is to forgive. We are exhorted to "forgive as the Lord forgave you" (Colossians 3:13).

People's propensity to complain and gripe can be traced to pressures often unrelated to the object of their criticism. Deep-seated pain over the way life has gone can easily breed a judgmental person. It may be an illness or financial failure or a career disappointment. Rejection, divorce, or abuse can breed an anger that turns everything into a complaint or a criticism. Those who feel under-appreciated, out of the loop, or in the way, are especially vulnerable. When frustration spills over, it can affect everything in life.

A critical spirit may say as much or more about the pressures we feel at work or the tensions in the office than the issue itself. Solving the petty complaint does not deal with the systemic problem, and the spirit of resentment and anger remains. Chronic complainers are often angry with God, even though they may be convinced they are defending God. Seldom do we find a chronic complainer from the ranks of those who are thrilled that God has forgiven them and blessed them with new life in Christ.

We can analyze a multitude of reasons as to why people are judgmental. And the exercise may be personally beneficial, even convicting, as long as the reasons do not become excuses. But we are better off admitting that we are taking our anger and frustration out on others. Wise is the person who seeks help, knowing how negative patterns in the past condition responses to people and situations now.

Judgmentalism can rob discipleship of joy and the household of faith of vitality. It is tragic when trivia occupies the mind and heart of a congregation. I know of one church that became overheated because of the pastor's insistence on wearing a turtleneck sweater under his suit coat on Sunday morning. This was back in the early seventies when pastors did such wild things. The congregation was impressed by the pastor's faithful and effective preaching. They even liked the man. He was a fine pastor and deeply spiritual. But some were embarrassed that their pastor wore a turtleneck instead of a tie. The debate raged on and the sweater became a symbol of the pastor's stubbornness. The opposition was led by a portly, rather aristocratic attorney who was never seen without a tie and coat. He even wore a tie to a Saturday morning elder's retreat in the country. For his part, the pastor reasoned that he wanted people who did not wear a tie to feel at home in the worship service. Tensions continued to build until the pastor finally left.

In his helpful book *Well-Intentioned Dragons: Ministering to Problem People*, Marshall Shelley observes:

> Perhaps the greatest damage done by true dragons is not their direct opposition. It's more intangible. They destroy enthusiasm, the morale so necessary for church health and growth. People no longer feel good about inviting friends to worship services. The air is tense, the church depressed, and everyone aware of "us" and "them."[5]

Somewhere along the line we have a choice to make. We can either sit back and criticize or we can minister to others. It is our choice whether we will allow peripheral issues to become fundamental issues. We can put our musical tastes, our special interests, our pet projects, and our self-recognition front and center, or we can learn to deny ourselves, take up our cross, and follow Him. We die to self in a thousand little ways. It's hard, but necessary.

On a sober note, sometimes the best thing that can happen to a congregation is a crisis, because a crisis calls us back to the centrality of Jesus Christ and the mission of the Church. It is often the hard times that allow the Body of Christ to refocus attention on why they are the Church in the first place.

FORCED EVANGELISM

Jesus refers to the third distortion cryptically, "Do not give to dogs what is sacred; do not throw your pearls to pigs." Those who succumb to this temptation force the gospel on others. Instead of living the gospel, they manipulate it.

At first glance, the warning against judging your brother appears to have no connection with casting pearls before pigs. But upon further reflection we see an important link. Those who persist in their judgmentalism forfeit their accessibility to the gospel. People who refuse to give up their critical spirit become dangerous people. Hooked on animosity, suspicion, and condemnation, they have neither the time nor the patience for the gospel. Such people are offended even by the best efforts to clear the air and make amends. They reject the initiative others take to bring about reconciliation as either manipulative or capitulating. They are blinded to the value of the truth, just as pigs are ignorant of the value of pearls. They are ready to tear apart the people who share with them the Word of God.

But didn't Jesus go to the cross for doing exactly that? Didn't He proclaim the gospel to those who ignored the truth and resented the good news? Surely, Jesus' warning was not meant to forbid preaching the gospel to unbelievers. Pastor John Stott rightly says, "To suppose this would stand the whole New Testament on its head and contradict the Great Commission (with which Matthew's Gospel ends) to 'go and make disciples of all nations.'"[6]

Throughout the history of the Church, the blood of martyrs

has watered the dry earth of unbelief. The message has been delivered not only in spite of, but even because of persecution. Sometimes where the opposition has been the fiercest, the determination of the Church has been the greatest. The warning by Jesus can hardly be used to dissuade the followers of Jesus from evangelism, but it can save believers the burden of subjecting the gospel to frivolous and unnecessary contempt. Bonhoeffer wrote,

> Every attempt to impose the gospel by force, to run after people and proselytize them, to use our own resources to arrange salvation of other people, is both futile and dangerous. It is futile, because the swine do not recognize the pearls that are cast before them, and dangerous, because it profanes the word of forgiveness, by causing those we fain would serve to sin against that which is holy.[7]

This warning pertains to both evangelism and spiritual direction, and it applies to those situations where we face the temptation of forcing the gospel upon those who have repeatedly expressed contempt for God. Jesus releases us from the burden of not taking "No" for an answer. It is wrong for the disciple to insist on acceptance when there is none. Bonhoeffer distinguishes between fanaticism and a passion for Christ. "An ideology requires fanatics, who neither know nor notice opposition . . . , but the Word of God in its weakness takes the risk of meeting the scorn of men and being rejected. There are hearts which are hardened and doors which are closed to the Word. The Word recognizes opposition when it meets it, and is prepared to suffer it."[8]

To pretend the gospel is received when it is actually spurned is to be dishonest. To change the gospel to fit the expectations of those who sit in judgment on it is wrong. Jesus did not run after the rich young ruler saying, "Let's make a deal."

This warning continues Jesus' commentary on the Lord's prayer, "Lead us not into temptation, but deliver us from evil." Throwing the gospel out without concern for how it will be received, or manipulating the gospel to assure some form of compromised acceptance, is to invite apostasy. Eugene Peterson picks up on this latter theme in his Bible translation, "Don't be flip with the sacred. Banter and silliness give no honor to God. Don't reduce holy mysteries to slogans. In trying to be relevant, you're only being cute and inviting sacrilege."[9] Bonhoeffer adds his concern, "Our easy trafficking with the word of cheap grace simply bores the world to disgust, so that in the end it turns against those who try to force on it what it does not want."[10]

Evangelism and spiritual direction were meant to be given with sensible regard for the people receiving the message. The disciple is free from the burden of forcing the message upon others, either through obnoxious insistence or manipulative enticement. The limitation is a necessary one for our spiritual health and authenticity.

PIOUS BABBLING

The fourth distortion turns communion with God into begging and babbling. Jesus now addresses the problem of pious performance. Prayer becomes begging when we seek to manipulate God through vain repetition, special pleading, or bargaining. Just before Jesus introduced the Lord's Prayer, He warned, "When you pray, do not keep on babbling like pagans, for they think they will be heard because of their many words. Do not be like them, for your Father knows what you need before you ask him" (Matthew 6:7).

We are tempted to look to God the way a panhandler zeros in on a tourist. Have you ever been approached by a street person and been impressed with how much of their tragic life story they can get out in thirty seconds? You feel like an easy target when they nab you and a fool when they walk away with your money. Those who minister to the street people of San

Diego tell us that giving cash is one of the worse things we could do. Giving money only encourages panhandling, fosters dependence, and often feeds an addiction. We are tempted to give in spite of the fact that we may feel lied to and intimidated. It should not surprise us that God does not operate that way.

God does not give to get rid of us or respond to our pleas against His better judgment. We are not panhandlers, begging for a handout, but children looking to our heavenly Father for His good gifts.

We don't coax God into doing something or impress Him with our sincerity. Prayer is as easy as asking and receiving, seeking and finding, ringing the doorbell and being welcomed with a handshake and an embrace. Don't embarrass yourself by acting like God is a tourist to be tricked or a wealthy uncle who needs to be appeased. You are not a minimum-wage employee asking the boss for a raise. "Don't bargain with God. Be direct. Ask for what you need. This isn't a cat-and-mouse, hide-and-seek game we're in."[11] God loves you the way the best kind of father loves his daughter and the best kind of mother loves her son. Simply ask, seek, and knock. "For everyone who asks receives; he who seeks finds; and to him who knocks, the door will be opened" (Matthew 7:8).

In conclusion, Jesus' easy yoke exposes the false dynamics that often accompany religious zeal: excessive worry, judgmentalism, manipulative evangelism, and pious performance. His commentary on the Lord's Prayer and His description of the "greater righteousness" (5:20) ends with a bottom line principle. "So in everything, do to others what you would have them do to you, for this sums up the Law and the Prophets" (7:12). It's as simple as it is profound and as comprehensive as it is practical: Put yourself in the other person's shoes and ask yourself what you want people to do for you. Then take the initiative to do it for them. Love them the way you want to be loved, correct them the way you want to be corrected. Comfort them the way you would like to be comforted. This is spiritual direction based on the gospel of reconciliation. It captures the essence of the Law and the Prophets. Jesus calls for simple obedience, humble devotion, and honest communion. Let's not make following Jesus more complicated than it needs to be. Jesus lightens the load and offers rest for the soul.

"*I*f you decide for God, living a life of God-worship, it follows that you don't fuss about what's on the table at mealtimes or whether the clothes in your closet are in fashion. There is far more to your life than the food you put in your stomach, more to your outer appearance than the clothes you hang on your body. Look at the birds, free and unfettered, not tied down to a job description, careless in the care of God. And you count far more to him than birds.

"Has anyone by fussing in front of the mirror ever gotten taller so much as an inch? All this time and money wasted on fashion—do you think it makes that much difference? Instead of looking at the fashions, walk out into the fields and look at the wildflowers. They never primp or shop, but have you ever seen color and design quite like it? The ten best-dressed men and women in the country look shabby alongside them.

"If God gives such attention to the appearance of wildflowers—most of which are never even seen—don't you think he'll attend to you, take pride in you, do his best for you? What I'm trying to do here is get you to relax, to not be so preoccupied with *getting*, so you can respond to God's *giving*. People who don't know God and the way he works fuss over these things, but you know both God and how he works. Steep your life in God-reality, God-initiative, God-provisions. Don't worry about missing out. You'll find all your everyday human concerns will be met.

"Give your entire attention to what God is doing right now, and don't get worked up about what may or may not happen tomorrow. God will help you deal with whatever hard things come up when the time comes."

MATTHEW 6:25-34, *THE MESSAGE*

"*D*on't pick on people, jump on their failures, criticize their faults—unless, of course, you want the same treatment. That critical spirit has a way of boomeranging. It's easy to see a smudge on your neighbor's face and be oblivious to the ugly sneer on your own. Do you have the nerve to say, 'Let me wash your face for you,' when your own face is distorted by contempt? It's this whole traveling road show mentality all over again, playing a holier-than-thou part instead of just living your part. Wipe that ugly sneer off your own face, and you might be fit to offer a washcloth to your neighbor.

"Don't be flip with the sacred. Banter and silliness give no honor to God. Don't reduce holy mysteries to slogans. In trying to be relevant, you're only being cute and inviting sacrilege.

"Don't bargain with God. Be direct. Ask for what you need. This isn't a cat-and-mouse, hide-and-seek game we're in. If your child asks for bread, do you trick him with sawdust? If he asks for fish, do you scare him with a live snake on his plate? As bad as you are, you wouldn't think of such a thing. You're at least decent to your own children. So don't you think the God who conceived you in love will be even better?

"Here is a simple, rule-of-thumb guide for behavior: Ask yourself what you want people to do for you, then grab the initiative and do it for *them*. Add up God's Law and Prophets and this is what you get."

MATTHEW 7:1-12, *THE MESSAGE*

"Enter through the narrow gate. For wide is the gate and broad is the road that leads to destruction, and many enter through it. But small is the gate and narrow the road that leads to life, and only a few find it.

"Watch out for false prophets. They come to you in sheep's clothing, but inwardly they are ferocious wolves. By their fruit you will recognize them. Do people pick grapes from thornbushes, or figs from thistles? Likewise every good tree bears good fruit, but a bad tree bears bad fruit. A good tree cannot bear bad fruit, and a bad tree cannot bear good fruit. Every tree that does not bear good fruit is cut down and thrown into the fire. Thus, by their fruit you will recognize them.

"Not everyone who says to me, 'Lord, Lord,' will enter the kingdom of heaven, but only he who does the will of my Father who is in heaven. Many will say to me on that day, 'Lord, Lord, did we not prophesy in your name, and in your name drive out demons and perform many miracles?' Then I will tell them plainly, 'I never knew you. Away from me, you evildoers!'

"Therefore everyone who hears these words of mine and puts them into practice is like a wise man who built his house on the rock. The rain came down, the streams rose, and the winds blew and beat against that house; yet it did not fall, because it had its foundation on the rock. But everyone who hears these words of mine and does not put them into practice is like a foolish man who built his house on sand. The rain came down, the streams rose, and the winds blew and beat against that house, and it fell with a great crash."

When Jesus had finished saying these things, the crowds were amazed at his teaching, because he taught as one who had authority, and not as their teachers of the law.

MATTHEW 7:13-29

CHAPTER THIRTEEN

How Easy Is Easy?

Jesus began His sermon with a benediction, "Blessed are the poor in spirit for theirs is the kingdom of heaven," and concluded with an exhortation, "Enter through the narrow gate. For wide is the gate and broad is the road that leads to destruction, and many enter through it. But small is the gate and narrow the road that leads to life, and only a few find it" (Matthew 7:13-14).

Modern preachers end positively; Jesus ended decisively, with layers of metaphor and admonition communicating a single message—a call for decision and action. Jesus closed with mini-summaries, word pictures, visualizing truth and comprehending the Message. Choose the narrow gate. Watch out for false prophets. Produce good fruit. Build your house on bedrock. His conclusion sounds more like John the Baptist, not Norman Vincent Peale. Judgment, delivered with urgency. "Every tree that does not bear good fruit is cut down and thrown into the fire" (verse 19). The final word is not a blessing but a warning. "The rain came down, the streams rose, and the winds blew and beat against that house, and it fell with a great crash" (verse 27).

CHOOSING THE NARROW GATE

By now anyone who has ears to hear understands that the call to a life of discipleship is not easy or popular in the worldly sense of easy. The admonition to "enter the narrow gate" should not surprise us. The contrast between the many and the few runs through the Sermon on the Mount. Neither the religious mainstream nor the secular majority find this narrow road that leads to life. The contrast is between a popular voice, "You have heard it said," and the voice of Jesus, "But I say to you." Jesus calls for a "greater righteousness." The narrow path introduces us to a whole new order of relationships, based not on alienation or the survival of the fittest, but on reconciliation. The grace of Christ sends us down a path that changes the way we live.

It's important to stress the obvious: The narrow gate does not imply that the way of discipleship is narrow-minded or exclusive. It may appear that way to those on Broadway simply because there is an alternative path and those who follow that path claim unequivocally that it is the way, the truth, and the life. The followers of Jesus have chosen the path of revelation instead of the highway of relativism. There is room for every kind of ideology, system, loyalty, and belief on the road that leads to destruction, but there is only room for truth on the way that leads to life. Anything goes on the road that leads nowhere.

Well-intentioned believers sometimes confuse the singularity of the gospel with the rigidity of religious systems. This was a problem in the early Church as well as in today's Church. Some Jewish-Christians wanted to impose the requirements of their religious tradition on Gentile-Christians. These requirements included ceremonial circumcision, dietary laws, honoring special feast days, etc.

The Apostle Peter, on the floor of the Jerusalem council, used the imagery of the yoke to reject this narrow-mindedness. "Now then, why do you try to test God by putting on the necks of the disciples a yoke that neither we nor our fathers have been able to bear?" He answered his own question with a resounding, "No! We believe it is through the grace of our Lord Jesus that we are saved, just as they are" (Acts 15:10-11). Years later, Peter and Paul would go head to head on this same issue. Only this time, it would be Peter succumbing to pressure to confuse the way of discipleship with religious forms and restrictions.

The narrowness of the gate that leads to life has to do with the disciple's single-minded, heartfelt commitment to following Jesus. It has nothing to do with limited seating in the Kingdom of Heaven. Everyone is invited to choose the small gate and narrow path and nowhere is it implied that the entrance is so crowded that people can't get in. Jeremiah, the prophet, offers the Lord's invitation, "Stand at the crossroads and look; ask for the ancient paths, ask where the good way is, and walk in it, and you will find rest for your souls" (Jeremiah 6:16).

Discipleship is total commitment, requiring everything else in life to be integrated with our devotion to Christ. There are no shortcuts. Again, following Jesus becomes a heavy burden when it is lived only part-time or when it is approached half-heartedly. Choosing the narrow path does not sound easy, but it is a whole lot easier than the alternative.

DISCERNING THE GOOD

Jesus weaves His conclusion with metaphors (gates, wolves, fruit trees) to stress a single meaning. The conclusion of the Sermon on the Mount calls us to act wisely because there are extraordinary consequences to our actions. We can choose the right path or the wrong path. We can lay the right foundation or the wrong one. Jesus would be remiss if He did not warn us that the responsibility to choose wisely, discern carefully, and act faithfully, was ours and ours alone. Nothing is said or implied here to ease the burden of choosing the easy yoke. Not even that God promises to guide and empower us to do the right thing. No mention is made here of the necessity of the Holy Spirit in our path-finding, decision-making, truth-discerning obedience, even though we know that to be absolutely true. The light burden of the easy yoke does not remove from our shoulders the responsibility to discern who is telling the truth and who is a wolf in sheep's clothing.

It's easy to be fooled if we're not careful. It's easy to be impressed by those who do their "acts of righteousness" in style, with an eye on the audience. Without meaning to, unsuspecting people fall victim to theatrics, envious of celebrity flair and excitement. It's natural to be drawn to those who appear to have the best of both worlds, those who have a "both/and" commitment to church things and material things. Powerful people, nice people, who seem equally devoted to God and money.

Jesus warned us away from such people. In the church there are bad preachers, just as in the orchard there are some bad trees. They may have good credentials and play the part, but don't be fooled. They are out to get you. They will exploit your emotions and pocketbook. Jesus assures us that, in time, "who's who" will be obvious, as obvious as a bad apple. But watch out between now and then; don't fall for them.

Discerning the counterfeit from the genuine article can be difficult, especially when they seem to have all the visible signs of spiritual power. But be assured of this, Jesus will not be fooled.

BUILDING ON BEDROCK

We might like an indecisive "maybe," the kind of middle-of-the-road Christianity practiced by the first church of Laodicea. But what we get instead are either/or alternatives: two ways (broad and narrow), two teachers (false and true), two pleas (words and deeds) and finally two foundations (sand and rock).[1] The Message ends on a parable about two kinds of builders: one who builds on the rock and one who builds on the sand. The contrast is between wisdom and foolishness.

Dependable contractors know the importance of building on the right foundation. Some of the larger buildings in our city rest on steel-reinforced concrete mats ten feet thick. Tons of concrete are poured continuously so no part of the foundation fails to adhere to the entire block. It is poured in and through a thick grid of steel re-bar so there will be no air pockets to weaken the mass. The taller the building, the deeper and more massive the foundation.

An Asian construction firm has designed an 1,800-foot (the Empire State Building is 1,200 feet), 121-story building, with concrete piles sunk 600 feet below ground. Without the right foundation, no matter how impressive the above-ground architecture, the building is not only worthless, but dangerous. It's what's below the surface that counts.

If Jesus were preaching the Message today, people would still be flipping mental channels, thinking about brunch or bridge or the bottom line. Going through the motions. Experts in verbal faith. Good Christians. Well versed in a knowledge about God, but with little knowledge of God. Living lives on the surface that resemble sand castles by the sea. Jesus warns against substituting rhetoric for righteousness, pious talk for commitment, and religious decorum for authentic spirituality. Faith in Christ is demonstrated through the works of faith. We are saved by faith alone, but saving faith is never alone. In the words of the Reformers, "Faith alone justifies, but not the faith that is alone." Luther put it well: "True faith will no more fail to produce good works than the sun can cease to give light."[2]

The sure sign of coming to Christ, taking His yoke, and learning from Him is to work the words of Jesus into our lives. The foundational words for our vocational life, friendships, passions, and priorities is the bedrock of Christ. The sandy soil of worried productivity and performance-based piety needs to be excavated so a whole new life can be built on a solid foundation.

Dire consequences await those who refuse to live under the easy yoke and practice the faith. The whole thing is so much more serious than we ever imagined. We thought we could live our superficial, distracted, fragmented lives without consequences. And then Jesus comes with the Message that must be obeyed. The small things add up, the pace of life speeds up, and before we know it, we've forgotten what Jesus had to say.

In a rush to get to work on time, a mother left her two-year-old boy asleep in the back seat of her locked van. It was August. The mother, a nurse at the McKee Medical Center in Denver, had planned to drop the child off at the daycare center on her way to work. She simply forgot, and once into her work routine the sleeping tot never crossed her mind.

Six hours later an emergency room physician smashed out a window with a hammer and rescued the child. The boy's temperature had reached 108 degrees. He never recovered consciousness and died within twenty-four hours. Charles Harms, the medical center's administrator, said the incident "reminds us that given the hectic pace at which most of us lead our lives today, critical events and twists can happen to any of us at any moment."

A more painful tragedy would be hard to imagine. The distraught parents were devastated. The newspapers discussed the possibility of charging the mother with involuntary manslaughter, but the judge determined that the mother's pain and suffering was far greater than any sentence the court could hand down. The little boy was left inadvertently, not intentionally. The mother was guilty of forgetting about her sleeping child, being preoccupied about work. The deadly consequence bore no relationship to the motives of the mother or the innocence of the negligence. Yet there is a cause and effect relationship, and the real world consequence has no excuse, only empathy. As Lance Morrow said, "The reality of reality always wins."[3]

When Jesus finished saying these things "the crowds were amazed at his teaching, because he taught as one who had authority and not as their teachers of the law" (Matthew 7:28-29). People could tell that Jesus knew what He was talking about. Straightforward, substance over style teaching. Convicting, not condemning; compelling, not controlling. They had never heard a rabbi tackle the everyday issues of lust and hate, anger and hypocrisy the way Jesus did. The reality of reality came through everything Jesus said and did.

Jesus was not like the modern-day sermon orator, the master of titillation and trivialization, who knows how to work the crowd, playing on their insecurities, triggering their emotions with patented techniques. It's hard to imagine Jesus knocking anybody's socks off with His rational, sit-down, think-about-it discourse. The Message did not "Wow!" the audience in the modern sense of the word "awesome," nor bypass the brain to get to the heart. Jesus used metaphors, not jokes; down-to-earth situations, not fancy fiction. When He finished, people were amazed at His teaching.

If you were there that day, would you have been amazed? Would you have been impressed by the authority of Jesus? I wonder. Do we have ears to hear what Jesus is saying to us today?

On November 19, 1863, President Lincoln went to Gettysburg to dedicate the new Union cemetery, but he was not the featured speaker. Edward Everett of Massachusetts, a diplomat, clergyman, and celebrated orator had the honors. The President was invited, as an afterthought, to offer a few appropriate remarks. Everett spoke for almost two hours. Then Lincoln rose to address the crowd. He spoke briefly, only 269 words. When he finished, people didn't know what to make of it. A few people applauded. The speech was over before it began. Even Lincoln thought he had failed.

The next day Lincoln and the speech were ridiculed in the *Chicago Times.* A speech that lasted less than two minutes, but a speech that emboldened the Union cause with some of the most stirring words ever spoken. They were healing words, words for everyone, for all time. They subsumed the entire war and all in it. They showed Lincoln's compassion and his love for his people.[4] It is fair to say that the original audience had no idea how significant that speech would become for the American people nor how historic that defining moment was in the life of the nation.

If we had sat on the hillside listening to Jesus, would we have been part of the crowd or would we have joined the disciples? Would the Message have shaped our strategy for living?

Many people are like the lawyer, Jake Brigance in John Grisham's novel *A Time to Kill*. Jake was raised a Methodist, and his wife, Carla, a Baptist. When they got married they became Presbyterian, a negotiated compromise that satisfied both of them. Baptist services went longer and Presbyterians usually got out in time to out race the rest of the church-going crowd to the restaurants for Sunday dinner. They were happy with their church and its activities and they seldom missed services.

On Sunday they sat in their usual pew and ignored the sermon. "Jake ignored it by watching the preacher and picturing" his upcoming trial case. "Carla ignored it by watching the preacher and mentally redecorating the dining room." Week after week, "Jake lied as he shook hands with the minister on the steps outside the sanctuary, 'Enjoyed your sermon, Reverend.'"[5]

Modern sermons have a way of easing us out the door into the virtual reality of business as usual. Somehow, I don't think people could listen to John the Baptist or the Apostle Paul and wonder if they would get a seat at the Fish Market for brunch or get home in time for the game.

I know a pastor who loves to use visual aids to get his point across. He has used bananas, balloons, and power tools, but people seldom remember what he is illustrating. Amusing anecdotes, human interest stories, and funny one-liners make for easy listening, but they don't help us to remember the truth. Memorable sermons, delivered and received without heartfelt convictions, become by Monday morning, forgettable. "Enjoyed your sermon, Reverend," is the polite thing to say.

Albert Einstein is quoted as saying, "Everything should be made as simple as possible, but not simpler."[6] All that we have studied about the easy yoke could be for naught if we drop the message at the end. Jesus is not about to let the sermon slip past us now. The Word is intrusive. The ball is in our court. Choice is unavoidable. Consequence is momentous. We don't just walk away saying, "Good sermon, Jesus, see You next week."

Apart from the grace of Christ and the saving work of the Cross, it would be impossible to convince people that the easy yoke is doable, let alone easy. But for those who live under the yoke there is absolutely no other way to live. Who in their right mind would go back to the gods of Self, Money, Lust and Power? Who would return on bended knee to the shrines of pious performance and judgmentalism? Is not love better than hate, purity better than lust, reconciliation better than retaliation? And is not "better" really "easier" when measured in character rather than convenience, rest for the soul rather than selfish pride?

In all our years of religion and church, are we missing something?

Have we ever experienced the reality of the easy yoke; discovered the rhythm of life, the rest of the soul, the lighter burden?

Do we know what it means to follow Jesus?

Jesus ends the Sermon on the Mount on a negative note. "Everyone who hears these words of Mine and puts them into practice is blessed, but the one who doesn't crashes. Amen." It's over. Time to go. He gets up to leave. This time it won't work to say, "Good sermon, Jesus, see You next week."

"*D*on't look for shortcuts to God. The market is flooded with surefire, easygoing formulas for a successful life that can be practiced in your spare time. Don't fall for that stuff, even though crowds of people do. The way to life—to God!—is vigorous and requires total attention.

"Be wary of false preachers who smile a lot, dripping with practiced sincerity. Chances are they are out to rip you off some way or other. Don't be impressed with charisma; look for character. Who preachers *are* is the main thing, not what they say. A genuine leader will never exploit your emotions or your pocketbook. These diseased trees with their bad apples are going to be chopped down and burned.

"Knowing the correct password—saying 'Master, Master,' for instance—isn't going to get you anywhere with me. What is required is serious obedience—*doing* what my Father wills. I can see it now—at the Final Judgment thousands strutting up to me and saying, 'Master, we preached the Message, we bashed the demons, our God-sponsored projects had everyone talking.' And do you know what I am going to say? 'You missed the boat. All you did was use me to make yourselves important. You don't impress me one bit. You're out of here.'

"These words I speak to you are not incidental additions to your life, homeowner improvements to your standard of living. They are foundational words, words to build a life on. If you work these words into your life, you are like a smart carpenter who built his house on solid rock. Rain poured down, the river flooded, a tornado hit—but nothing moved that house. It was fixed to the rock.

"But if you just use my words in Bible studies and don't work them into your life, you are like a stupid carpenter who built his house on the sandy beach. When a storm rolled in and the waves came up, it collapsed like a house of cards."

When Jesus concluded his address, the crowd burst into applause. They had never heard teaching like this. It was apparent that he was living everything he was saying—quite a contrast to their religion teachers! This was the best teaching they had ever heard.

Matthew 7:13-29, *The Message*

NOTES

CHAPTER 1—WHO STOLE THE EASY YOKE?

1. Barbara W. Tuchman, *A Distant Mirror: The Calamitous Fourteenth Century* (New York: Ballantine Books, 1978).
2. C. S. Lewis, *Surprised by Joy* (London: Fontana Books, 1955), pp. 182-183.
3. Dietrich Bonhoeffer, *The Cost of Discipleship* (New York: Macmillan, 1963), pp. 47-48.
4. Gary Smith, "As Time Runs Out," *Sports Illustrated* (January 11, 1993), pp. 11-25.
5. Sören Kierkegaard, quoted in Dallas Willard, *The Spirit of the Disciplines* (San Francisco, Harper & Row, 1988), p. 1.
6. Bonhoeffer, *The Cost of Discipleship,* p. 48.

CHAPTER 2—HAPPINESS IS SERIOUS BUSINESS

1. Neil Postman, *Technopoly: The Surrender of Culture to Technology* (New York: Alfred A. Knopf, 1992), p. 164.
2. Dietrich Bonhoeffer, *The Cost of Discipleship,* p. 37.
3. Dallas Willard, *The Spirit of the Disciplines,* p. 10.
4. Donald W. McCullough, *Finding Happiness in the Most Unlikely Places* (Downers Grove, IL: InterVarsity Press, n.d.), p. 23.
5. *Theological Dictionary of the New Testament,* vol. 4

(Grand Rapids, MI: Eerdmans, 1967), p. 362.

6. Earl Palmer, *The Enormous Exception* (Waco, TX: Word Books, 1986), p. 22.

7. McCullough, pp. 37-38.

8. Charles Colson, *The Body* (Dallas: Word, 1992), pp. 189-191.

9. C. S. Lewis, *Surprised by Joy,* p. 181.

10. James I. Packer, "Pleasure Principles," *Christianity Today* (November 22, 1993), p. 26.

11. McCullough, p. 24.

CHAPTER 3—FROM BLAME TO BLESSING

1. Charles J. Sykes, *A Nation of Victims: The Decay of the American Character* (New York: St. Martin's Press, 1992), p. 11.

2. Sykes, p. 41.

3. George Will, "An Evil Act Deserves Swift, Severe Punishment," *Sunday Herald-Times* (April 30, 1989), p. A12.

4. Paul Ciotti, "If the Menendez Boys Aren't Guilty, Then No One Is," *Union-Tribune* (January 27, 1994).

5. Barbara Tuchman, *The Distant Mirror*, p. 101.

6. David Meyers, *The Other Side* (April 1982), p. 30.

7. John L. Mitchell and David Ferrell, "Faal Emerging from Denny Case as Rising Legal Star," *Los Angeles Times* (April 17, 1994), pp. A1, A18.

8. C. S. Lewis, *Mere Christianity* (Glasgow, Scotland: Collins, 1978), p. 80.

9. Robert A. Guelich, *The Sermon on the Mount: A Foundation for Understanding* (Waco, TX: Word, 1982), p. 81.

CHAPTER 4—WILLED PASSIVITY

1. Donald W. McCullough, *Finding Happiness in the Most Unlikely Places,* p. 61.

2. Rollo May, quoted by Ronald Rottschafer, "The Passive Christian," *The Reformed Journal* (December 1983), pp. 11-12.

3. Eugene H. Peterson, "Growth: An Act of the Will," *Leadership* (Fall 1988), p. 40.
4. See Eugene H. Peterson, *A Long Obedience in the Same Direction* (Downers Grove, IL: InterVarsity Press, 1980), p. 105.
5. Eugene H. Peterson, *Reversed Thunder: The Revelation of John and the Praying Imagination* (San Francisco: Harper & Row, 1988), p. 117.
6. D. Martyn Lloyd-Jones, *Studies in the Sermon on the Mount* (Grand Rapids, MI: Eerdmans, 1972), p. 71.
7. Derek Kidner, *Psalms 1-72: An Introduction & Commentary* (Downers Grove, IL: InterVarsity Press, 1973), p. 149.
8. Peterson, *Reversed Thunder*, p. 125.

CHAPTER 5—SALT AND LIGHT DISCIPLES

1. John Wesley, *The Works of the Rev. John Wesley*, vol. V (London: Wesleyan Conference Office, 1878), p. 301.
2. Tim Stafford, "Move Over: ACLU," *Christianity Today* (October 25, 1993), p. 20.
3. Dietrich Bonhoeffer, *The Cost of Discipleship* (New York: Macmillan, 1963), p. 130.
4. R.E.O. White, *Christian Ethics* (Atlanta: John Knox Press, 1981), p. 19.
5. White, *Christian Ethics*, p. 19.
6. White, *Christian Ethics*, p. 20.
7. John R. W. Stott, *Christian Counter-Culture: The Message of the Sermon on the Mount* (Downers Grove, IL: InterVarsity Press, 1978), p. 64.
8. Helmut Thielicke, *Life Can Begin Again: Sermons on the Sermon on the Mount*, John W. Doberstein, trans. (Philadelphia, PA: Fortress, 1963), p. 28.
9. Eugene H. Peterson, *A Long Obedience in the Same Direction*, pp. 70-71.
10. Charles L. Glenn, "Why Public Schools Don't Listen," *Christianity Today* (September 20, 1985), pp. 13-16.
11. Thomas Elkins, "A Legacy of Life," *Christianity Today*

(January 18, 1985), pp. 18-26.

12. Elkins, "A Legacy of Life," pp. 18-26.

13. Jeff Barneson and Michael Knosp, "The Harvard Evangelical Laity Involvement Exercises (HELIX)," unpublished material.

14. Stott, *Christian Counter-Culture,* p. 60.

CHAPTER 6—SETTING THE RECORD STRAIGHT

1. Dietrich Bonhoeffer, *The Cost of Discipleship,* p. 54.

2. R. T. France, *Jesus and the Old Testament* (Downers Grove, IL: InterVarsity, 1971), p. 114.

3. E. Ferguson, "Marcion," *Evangelical Dictionary of Theology,* Walter Elwell, ed. (Grand Rapids, MI: Baker, 1984), p. 685.

4. France, *Jesus and the Old Testament,* p. 115.

5. Eugene H. Peterson, *The Message: The New Testament in Contemporary Language* (Colorado Springs, CO: NavPress, 1993), p. 17.

6. C. S. Lewis, *Miracles* (New York: Macmillan, 1947), pp. 113-114.

7. Walter Wangerin, *As For Me and My House* (Nashville: Thomas Nelson Publishers, 1987), p. 8.

8. John R. W. Stott, *Christian Counter-Culture,* p. 75.

9. E. Stanley Jones, *The Christ of the Mount* (London: Hodder & Stoughton, 1931), p. 29.

CHAPTER 7—VISIBLE RIGHTEOUSNESS

1. R. T. France, *Jesus and the Old Testament,* pp. 119-120.

2. Robert A. Guelich, *The Sermon on the Mount,* p. 240.

3. John Perkins, *A Quiet Revolution* (Waco, TX: Word Books, 1976), pp. 190-91.

CHAPTER 8—JESUS ON SEX

1. Tom Wolfe, *The Bonfire of the Vanities* (New York: Farrar, Straus, Giroux, 1987), p. 54.

2. Tim Stafford, *The Sexual Christian* (Wheaton, IL: Victor

Books, 1989), p. 59.

3. C. S. Lewis, *The Four Loves* (London: Harcourt Brace Jovanovich, 1960), p. 138.

4. James Patterson and Peter Kim, *The Day America Told the Truth* (New York: Plume, 1992), pp. 94-99.

5. John R. W. Stott, *Christian Counter-Culture,* p. 87.

6. Paul A. Mickey, "Get Rid of the Lust in Your Life," *TSF Bulletin* (March-April 1986), p. 11.

7. Stafford, *The Sexual Christian,* pp. 17-31.

8. Anne Wilson Schaef, *When Society Becomes an Addict* (San Francisco: Harper & Row, 1987), pp. 22-23.

9. Stafford, *The Sexual Christian,* p. 39.

10. Robert A. Guelich, *The Sermon on the Mount,* pp. 242-43.

11. Guelich, *The Sermon on the Mount,* p. 194.

12. John R. W. Stott, *Christian Counter-Culture,* p. 89.

13. Peter Kreeft, *Back to Virtue: Traditional Moral Wisdom For Modern Moral Confusion* (San Francisco: Ignatius Press, 1992), p. 169.

14. Walter Wangerin, *As For Me and My House,* p. 195

15. Wangerin, *As For Me and My House,* p. 196.

16. Wangerin, *As For Me and My House,* p. 195.

17. Stafford, *The Sexual Christian,* pp. 11-12.

CHAPTER 9—SIMPLE HONESTY

1. William Willimon, *The Intrusive Word* (Grand Rapids, MI: Eerdmans, 1994), pp. 74-77.

2. E. Stanley Jones, *The Christ of the Mount,* p. 140.

3. Lewis B. Smedes, *Mere Morality* (Grand Rapids, MI: Eerdmans, 1983), p. 211.

4. Niccolo Machiavelli, *The Prince,* trans. James B. Atkinson (Indianapolis: Bobbs-Merrill Educational Publishing, 1976), p. 257.

5. Machiavelli, *The Prince,* p. 279.

6. Machiavelli, *The Prince,* p. 281.

7. Stephen Westerholm, *Jesus and Scribal Authority*

(Doctoral Thesis at Lund University: CWK Gleerup, 1978), p. 105.

8. Cheryl Forbes, *The Religion of Power* (Grand Rapids, MI: Zondervan, 1983), p. 86.

9. Robert A. Guelich, *The Sermon on the Mount,* p. 250.

10. Dietrich Bonhoeffer, *The Cost of Discipleship,* pp. 154-55.

11. Walter Wangerin, *As For Me And My House*, p. 123.

12. Wangerin, *As For Me And My House*, p. 123.

13. Wangerin, *As For Me And My House*, p. 122.

14. Wangerin, *As For Me And My House*, p. 123.

15. Dietrich Bonhoeffer, *The Cost of Discipleship,* p. 155.

CHAPTER 10—HIDDEN RIGHTEOUSNESS

1. Dietrich Bonhoeffer, *The Cost of Discipleship,* p. 172.

2. Georg Huntemann, *The Other Bonhoeffer: An Evangelical Reassessment of Dietrich Bonhoeffer* (Grand Rapids, MI: Baker Books, 1993), p. 101. Huntemann quotes from Bonhoeffer's lecture entitled, "Thy Kingdom Come," given in Potsdam, November 19, 1932.

3. Huntemann, *The Other Bonhoeffer*, p. 108.

4. Eugene H. Peterson, *The Message: Psalms* (Colorado Springs, CO: NavPress, 1994), p. 75.

5. Eugene H. Peterson, *The Message,* p. 19.

6. Peterson, *The Message,* p. 19.

7. Eugene H. Peterson, *Psalms,* pp. 5-6.

8. C. S. Lewis, *The Weight of Glory* (New York: Collier Books, 1949), p. 4.

9. Lewis, *The Weight of Glory*, p. 4.

10. Earl F. Palmer, *The Enormous Exception,* p. 61.

CHAPTER 11—VALUES, VISION, AND LOYALTIES

1. Robert A. Guelich, *The Sermon on the Mount,* p. 363.

2. Guelich, *The Sermon on the Mount,* p. 328.

3. Eugene H. Peterson, *The Message,* p. 20.

4. Dietrich Bonhoeffer, *The Cost of Discipleship,* p. 195.

5. C. S. Lewis, *The Weight of Glory,* pp. 4-5.

CHAPTER 12—LIGHTEN UP

1. Dietrich Bonhoeffer, *The Cost of Discipleship,* p. 208.
2. Os Guinness, "More Victimized Than Thou," in *No God But God: Breaking with the Idols of Our Age* (Chicago: Moody Press, 1992), p. 88.
3. Robert A. Guelich, *The Sermon on the Mount,* p. 336.
4. William Willimon, *The Intrusive Word,* pp. 61-62.
5. Marshall Shelley, *Well-Intentioned Dragons: Ministering to Problem People in the Church* (Waco, TX: Word Books, 1985), p. 41.
6. John R. W. Stott, *Christian Counter-Culture,* p. 182.
7. Dietrich Bonhoeffer, *The Cost of Discipleship,* p. 206.
8. Bonhoeffer, *The Cost of Discipleship,* p. 207.
9. Eugene H. Peterson, *The Message,* pp. 21-22.
10. Dietrich Bonhoeffer, *The Cost of Discipleship,* p. 207.
11. Peterson, *The Message,* p. 22.

CHAPTER 13—HOW EASY IS EASY?

1. John R. W. Stott, *Christian Counter-Culture,* p. 193.
2. Donald G. Bloesch, *Essentials of Evangelical Theology,* vol.1 (San Francisco: Harper & Row, 1978), pp. 223-252.
3. Lance Morrow, "Living in Virtual Reality," *TIME* (May 16, 1994), p. 94.
4. Rick Burns, Producer, *The Civil War* (Florentine Films), PBS series.
5. John Grisham, *A Time to Kill* (New York: Doubleday, 1989), p. 118.
6. Peggy Anderson, ed., *Great Quotes from Great Leaders* (Glendale Heights, CA: Celebrating Excellence, 1989), p. 13.

ACKNOWLEDGMENTS

I am extremely grateful to Cherry Creek Presbyterian Church in Denver, to the Country Network Bible School in Mongolia, and First Presbyterian Church in San Diego for helping to create this book. Both Kathy Yanni and Liz Heaney of NavPress were easy to work with. Kathy is a happy, positive person, who saw the potential of the project, and Liz's editorial gifts strengthened my ability to communicate the message. Writing takes on special significance for me, because of Jeremy, Andrew, and Kennerly Webster, who remind me daily how important it is for their father to live under the easy yoke of Jesus. I am very thankful for Ginny who shares each step of the journey and lightens the load (Ecclesiastes 4:9-10). If marriage is a good analogy for our partnership with Christ, then in Ginny I have had every advantage in seeing more clearly the value of being yoked to Christ.

AUTHOR

Doug Webster is the pastor of First Presbyterian Church in San Diego, California. He has authored several books, including *A Passion For Christ*, *Finding Spiritual Direction*, and *Selling Jesus*. Doug and his wife, Ginny, have three children, Jeremy, Andrew, and Kennerly.